CRUSH YOUR OBSTACLES

CRUSH YOUR OBSTACLES

A 10 Step Guide to Transforming Your Mind and Money Habits with Tapping

MARY CASSIDY

Hudson Coffey Press
Livingston, Montana

Copyright© 2019 by Mary Cassidy

All rights reserved. This book may not be reproduced in whole or in part without written permission from the publisher, except by a reviewer who may quote brief passages in a review; nor may any part of this book be reproduced, stored in a retrieval system or transmitted in any form or by any means, electronic, mechanical, photocopying, recording or other, without written permission from the publisher.

Published by Hudson Coffey Press
Livingston, Montana

Editing by Jessica Vineyard, Red Letter Editing, LLC
Cover and interior design by Christy Collins, Constellation Book Services

Printed in the United States of America

Publisher's Cataloging-in-Publication Data

Names: Cassidy, Mary Pierson, author.

Title: Crush your obstacles : a 10 step guide to transforming your mind and money habits with tapping / Mary Cassidy.

Description: Includes bibliographical references. | Livingston, MT: Hudson Coffey Press, 2019.

Identifiers: ISBN 978-1-7337036-0-4 (pbk.) | 978-1-7337036-1-1 (ebook)

Subjects: LCSH Acupuncture points--Therapeutic use. | Self-actualization (Psychology) | Finance, Personal. | Change (Psychology) | Habit-breaking. | Money--Psychological aspects. | BISAC BUSINESS & ECONOMICS / Personal Success | SELF-HELP / Anxieties & Phobias | PSYCHOLOGY / Emotions

Classification: LCC HG179 .C348 2019 | DDC 332.024--dc23

Dedication

To Jesus, my Hulk on all levels; my children, Maria Kuklinski, Raphael and Jennifer Pierson, and Hannah and Ian Cook. To Maren, Emmie, Ella, and little ones coming soon. To my mother and best friend, Mary Coffey Pierson, and her dad, Charles Hudson Coffey, aka "Boppy."

Contents

Introduction	1
Quick Start Guide	7
Chapter 1: Story	15
Chapter 2: Tapping	25
Chapter 3: Resolve	33
Chapter 4: Own	39
Chapter 5: VAKOG	49
Chapter 6: RAS	65
Chapter 7: Competence	77
Chapter 8: Focus	85
Chapter 9: Persevere	93
Chapter 10: Believe	101
Chapter 11: Receive	109
Epilogue	119
Appendix	121
Glossary	125
Resources	129
Notes	133

Gratitude

Thank you, God, for making me do this project and showing me that I can do all things through you. Maria, pursuing greatness really began with motherhood and you. Raphael, thank you for being brave growing up in a family of strong women and for your willingness to believe in all that's good! And Hannah, thank you for being you. Your tender ability to acknowledge and encourage the underdog in life humbles me. Thank you for feeding me all the little love notes you leave hidden after a visit. Jen and Ian, I am grateful and honored to call you daughter and son. You add rich dimension to our lives.

Thanks to my dear friends and clients for trusting and loving your way through "the terrain of the heart" with me. I learn much from you. Deep thanks to Robert G. Smith, the founder of FasterEFT/Eutaptics; Richard Bandler and John Grinder, co-creators of NLP; Gary Craig for EFT; and Jack Canfield and Brené Brown for inspiring greatness in self and others. Steve Harrison, Martha Bullen, all my Quantum Leap coaches, Margherita Harrington thank you for your superb support, guidance and championing.

Shift
By Mary Cassidy

Walking down the street, there is a depression in the sidewalk . . . Will it suck me in? Do I let it again?

Pause. I open the door in the middle of my chest. Swirling galaxies and starry masses sing my name free.

Shift. I grab the sidewalk, shake it like an old woman's carpet, smile, and walk on my way.

Whether you think you can or you think you can't—you're right.
—HENRY FORD

Introduction

My story of money habits and obstacles started the way most people's do: in my own family. For me, money equaled self-worth. That is what this story is about: transforming my self-worth (which starts in the mind), which then transformed my experience with money. I grew up with parents who thought a certain way about themselves and about money. Their ideas affected me, as all of us are affected by our parents' ideas, habits, and words.

For most of my life, I had an unproductive philosophy about money: there wasn't enough, and it wasn't my fault. I made good choices and bad. I married, had children, divorced, and raised the children as a single parent. I dreamt of a prosperity mindset, an external experience of plenty, but the pervasive not-enough-money pattern was chronic. I didn't know money was related to low self-worth. I continually sought answers to this dilemma of behavioral economics, but unconsciously, I blamed my financial status on being a single parent and not having enough time, money, or energy to manage all the puzzle pieces. *I unconsciously blamed.* This was the root of the pattern, and when I finally realized it, the door to prosperity in me unlocked.

With my children grown and the money pattern of not-enough persisting, I finally acknowledged that the problem was in me and my thinking. If there was anyone to blame, it was me. I dug in and accepted personal responsibility. It wasn't particularly pleasant or easy. I had to wade through shame, the murky waters that could flood me in an instant and topple my commitment.

I devoted time and money to doing the internal work. I hadn't realized yet that I would have to radically change my perception of myself. Professor and author Brené Brown has done seminal research and written extensively on courage, vulnerability, shame, and empathy, and reading her books helped me immensely. A quote from her homepage says it all: "The bottom line: I believe you have to walk through vulnerability to get to courage, therefore . . . embrace the suck."[1]

I used to run from vulnerability because vulnerability meant weakness. I now "embrace the suck" to remind myself to embrace the discomfort and keep putting one foot in front of the other in this new mindfulness endeavor. "Embrace the suck" is also used in the military to acknowledge the hard stuff and move through it anyway. Now I have words to convey the experience of transforming myself and creating a money mindset.

> People who wade into discomfort and vulnerability and tell the truth about their stories are the real badasses.
> —BRENÉ BROWN

Intense introspection takes courage. Learning and changing behavior takes bravery. Through her books (*Daring Greatly*, *Rising Strong*, *Dare to Lead*, and others), Brown was one of my mentor-companions who championed my mission to change my money habits by changing myself. The tool I used to change my beliefs, feelings, and memories (BFMs) was tapping. Brown doesn't know it, but her books urged me on through steep terrain. Shame was a tangible threat. It made me weak and want to give up; sometimes it still does. I think of shame as an internal tornado that produces an external "suck zone," where anything and everything in its path is devoured, destroyed, or marred, including people, places, and things, when the conditions are just right. In the 1996 movie *Twister*, a tornado chaser named Dusty describes the tornado suck zone of an F5 tornado to a novice storm chaser: "It's the point basically at which the twister sucks you up. That's not the technical term for it, obviously." Shame, twisters, and the suck zone. This sums up my experience on bad days during childhood.

When the grownups in my world were flooded by it, shame was a twister, a force of nature that no one could control, not even little Mary. So, instead of feeling shame, I became it. Only later did I learn that shame is technically a feeling, not an identity. But for me, growing up in an alcoholic home, it was more.

In my family, shame was a huge data set consisting of beliefs, feelings, and memories. It was passed like a hot potato from parent to parent, parent to child, child to child, to grandparents, and to anyone else in my formative world. Like all kids, I watched, listened, and learned. Wading through my ongoing adult experience of not-enough-money, I had to dig deep and find the courage to deal with the shame zone inside, dismantle it like a sophisticated bomb, and figure out how it was related to money.

My money habits were born in that twister, and I was determined to extract the truth, change myself, and let the rest go. It was during this grappling that I found the self-help tool called the Emotional Freedom Technique (EFT), also known as tapping. I started using tapping and got help from an EFT practitioner. It worked, but progress was slow. Since I was actively addressing the emotional twister from childhood, I needed help fast. That F5 tornado was intense, I felt emotionally unequipped, and I was afraid I might die trying to figure everything out. Then I found FasterEFT/Eutaptics, a tool that works in the moment and takes the wind out of shame.

I had been fighting that invisible twister for so long that I no longer knew what it was like to feel peace for a moment or two. Through tapping, I learned to interrupt the strong flood of shame that would wash over me, and I started to make serious progress. I could tell because I felt more space inside me, and I could finally breathe. Even though I was wading through emotional yuck, I felt freer. Tapping quieted me, and self-acceptance started to creep in. During my FasterEFT home study course training, I finally understood, on a gut level, that the past was over. It was done.

When I discovered that I had been hurting myself by denying, reviewing, talking about, and running from my past, I felt sad, ashamed, and full of regret that I had learned to hurt myself in this way. I would think, *What? I'm doing it to myself? That can't be.* I had been kicking my own financial butt by the thoughts I had been thinking about myself, money, and the world, so before I could make serious changes, I had to get past the shock and disgust I felt about being responsible for creating my emotional and financial experiences of scarcity and lack. I wish I could say that I got through this stage quickly, but I was flooded by confusion and self-loathing. In retrospect, I believe I was processing not only shame but also the entire gamut of grief: anger, denial, bargaining, depression, and finally, acceptance.

Once I accepted that my money habits were self-initiated patterns of thought based on low self-worth, I got busy changing my mind. My litany of excuses and defenses would rise to the surface, but one by one, I tapped out the beliefs, feelings, and memories that supported the shame. They had been fuel for the twister, and once I stopped fueling the shame, progress came fast. Using this new tool of tapping, I neutralized old emotions and "tapped in" good beliefs of safety, belonging, and having enough. Finally, I was out of the twister suck zone, and I could think again.

To me, tapping is an intellectual approach to feelings. It brings me comfort to know that I have the tools to diffuse overwhelming emotions, beliefs, and feelings in the moment, whether they are about me or my money habits. Jack Canfield's book *The Success Principles* gave me new filters that, when applied to my thoughts along with tapping, allowed me to start changing my self-perception and from there, my money habits. I consider a mindset to be a series of habitual thoughts we unconsciously enact that produce a specific result, and with diligent practice, these new habits became my new mindset.

I trust you will get something out of reading my story. I wrote it to heal myself, share hope, and start a revolution of self-change with tapping. My biggest takeaway from writing *Crush Your Obstacles* is that perception is everything and that

I am personally responsible for mine. Shame, post-traumatic stress disorder (PTSD), and money issues had commingled to form a personal, character-building challenge that taught me perseverance, compassion, and courage. With dogged determination, I found tapping to be a solution for abiding emotional and monetary change. It has freed me from shame, the unproductive habits of mind we call PTSD, feelings of low self-worth, and the adverse economic impact of replaying bad stories in my head. I thank God for the opportunity to heal.

As a result of the changes I have made to my thought habits, I created this ten-step guide to transforming mind and money habits by using tapping. The book integrates myriad cutting-edge information, and with dedication and practice, you will see a transformation in your mind and your finances. A worksheet follows each chapter, so you will want to answer the questions and do the work, as it will help you to change your thought habits and incorporate new ways of thinking.

I have complete confidence that the information in this guide will help you as it helped me. Perhaps you will see yourself in parts of this writing, receive inspiration, and learn a new tool to use in your own life. Whatever you receive, I wish you oceans of prosperity, inside and out.

Quick Start Guide

If you have an immediate need to tap and want to get started right now, here are ten simplified actions to take. A worksheet is provided at the end of this quick-start guide. I will unpack the concepts and my experience throughout the rest of the book.

Day-to-day experiences and seasonal events bring up beliefs, feelings, and memories (BFMs) from the past; these are known as "thought habits" and are normal. Technically, of course, the past is over. Previously lived moments cannot be accessed unless we replay them in our minds through pictures, sounds, feelings, smells, and tastes. This access is called "VAKOG," an acronym for the visual, auditory, kinesthetic, olfactory and gustatory ways that we process information. VAKOG is a neuro-linguistic programming (NLP) term coined by Richard Bandler and John Grinder, co-creators of NLP.* Essentially, the pictures, sounds, and feelings we hold inside are the ways in which we represent our lives, loves, and experiences.

---

* NLP is a comprehensive approach to communication, personal development, and psychotherapy. To learn more about it, see the entry for neurolinguistic programming at *Wikipedia*: https://en.wikipedia.org/wiki/Neuro-linguistic_programming.

VAKOG quickly informs our opinions and perceptions—which lead to our thoughts and feelings—in the moment and produces our personal version of life. Our version of life is what causes our stress, and everyone experiences stress in different ways. For example, consider a common annual money event such as tax season. Some people address financial record keeping throughout the year and proceed through tax season feeling neutral about it, while others anticipate April 15 with procrastination or dread. Tapping can help with these feelings. This guide will show you how to use tapping to change stressful beliefs, feelings, and memories. With practice, you will be able to let these old BFMs go, feel better, and quickly transform your mental habits of self and money.

What Is Tapping?

Tapping is a do-it-yourself stress-relief tool based on the five-thousand-year-old practice of Chinese acupuncture. This ancient practice uses meridians, which run throughout the body and connect various points in the hands, feet, arms, and legs to the body organs. When stress arises, we tap these meridians on four points of the face. The act of tapping releases stress by interrupting our VAKOG (pictures, sounds, mental movies, feelings) and positively altering our neural processes about the stress.

How to Tap

Follow the actions below to see how to start tapping.

Action 1: Identify a stressor.

You know what stress is, and you know what money is. Identify a money stressor, such as a bill coming due or a chronic worry. Name the stressor. Write it down as a brief, bold newspaper headline. For example, "Not enough money to go to the concert next month."

Action 2: Determine how you know you are stressed.
How do you know you are stressed? Do you experience your stress as a picture, a movie, a sound, or a feeling? Do you have a feeling in the gut, a pain in the head, thoughts swirling in your mind, internal monologue, or nonstop self-talk? However you are experiencing stress, this is your personal VAKOG telling you *how* to be stressed about this money situation. Write down how you know you are stressed.

Action 3: Determine your earliest memory of a stressful money experience.
Recall the earliest memory you can of when you experienced a stress about money. It's best to use the oldest memory you can recall because that one has been around the longest, and you are probably good at reproducing that stress in your body as a result of repetition. Once you have identified it, name it. For example, "Not enough money to go to state fair, middle school."

Action 4: Rate the stress.
To identify the level of stress you feel, use the Subjective Units of Distress Scale (SUDS), where 0 = no stress and 10 = high stress.* Rate the current money stressor from action 1, and write that number next to the headline you wrote down. Then rate the memory you identified in action 3, and write that number down, too.

---

* The SUDS rating scale was developed by Joseph Wolpe in 1969.

With this subjective rating scale, you are in charge. In the next action, as you tap on your earliest memory, your stress will decrease for the current stress, too. Tapping changes your perception of stress and the thought habits that created it. What you measure, moves, and using SUDS to measure gives you instant access to your stress level so you can change it yourself. Master this, and you will be in the transformation zone. You will know, at any given moment in time, how stressed you are on a scale of 0 to 10. You can also know where and how you feel that stress in your body, and then change it using action 5.

Action 5: Tap.
You have identified and rated your money stress, and now it's time to change it. Using two fingers, tap several times on the following points: between your eyebrows, on the sides of your eyes, under your eyes, and on your collarbone (see fig. 1).

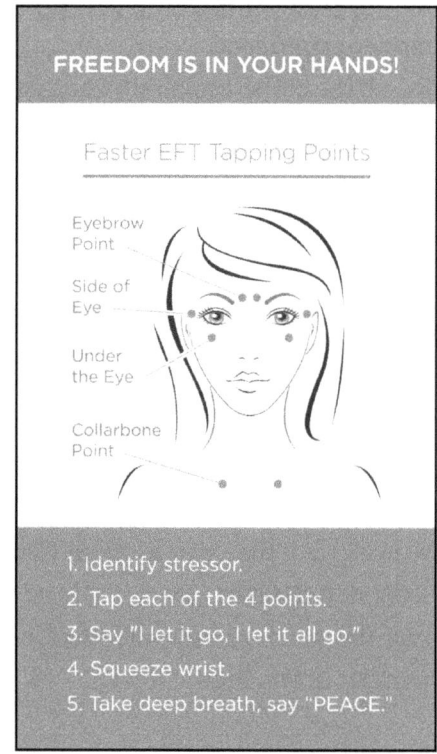

Figure 1: Tapping points

As you tap, say "let it go," aloud or in your mind, at each point. Then take a deep breath, squeeze your wrist, and say "peace." This is one round of tapping.

Action 6: Rate the stress again.
You identified a stressor in action 1 and then assigned it a number prior to the first round of tapping. Each time you complete a round, the stress will be lower, and the number you assign it will be lower. The stress will drop even more quickly after you do action 7 before starting another round.

What number is the stress now? 0 = no stress, 10 = high stress. Write it down.

Action 7: Think of a happy, peaceful memory.
See, hear, or feel a memory that makes you feel really good. It can be completely unrelated to money. Using the SUDS of 0 = not at all happy and 10 = super happy, find a memory that rates a 10. Think of the memory, take a breath, and say "peace."

Action 8: Continue tapping and rating.
Continue with tapping rounds (actions 5 and 6), going to your happy, peaceful memory between rounds (action 7), until your stress response to the earliest money memory reaches zero. Once this memory is at zero, check the SUDS rating on your current money stress. Rate it, and continue to tap until it reaches zero.

Action 9: Tap *in* something you prefer to experience.
You have now neutralized your perceptions and feelings about the money stress you started with, so it's time to "tap in" something better—often the opposite of the earliest memory.

For example, "Not enough money to go to state fair, middle school" can change to "I found ten bucks! State fair was a blast!" Imagine a scene of yourself having a blast, the sounds of the fair, your friends' voices, and so on. Make up a positive scene, and imagine *great* feelings inside your body. Imagine that this scene is happening in real time.

Tap *in* your preferred memory while you picture or feel it at each of the tapping points. Then take a deep breath, squeeze your wrist, and say, "peace." (I often replace "peace" with an affirmation about the new experience: "I had such a great time in middle school. Going to that state fair was epic.") At the end of tapping in your preferred experience, go to your happy memory. Another quick little dose of feeling good creates layers to a positive feeling state.

Action 10: Check the original stress.

Close your eyes and attempt to locate the original stress in your body. Can you find it? Are there any negative pictures, sounds, or feelings left? If so, rate them, and then do more rounds of tapping until the stress is zero. Do the same for your earliest memory. Can you find it, or has it changed to neutral? If there is any emotion left, tap it out. When both the current and the earliest money memories are at zero, go back to action 9 and tap in your preferred money experience. That's it!

Quick-Start Worksheet

Action 1: Identify a stressor. Give it a name, and write it here.
_____

Action 2: Determine how you know. Is it a picture, a movie, dialogue, feelings, or sensations in your body? Write down how you know.
_____
_____

Action 3: Determine your earliest memory of a similar stressor. Give it a name, and write it down here.
_____
_____

Action 4: Rate the earliest memory stressor using the Subjective Units of Distress Scale (SUDS), where 0 = no stress and 10 = high stress. Write the number down here._____

Action 5: Tap.

Action 6: Rate the stressor again, and write the number down here._____

Action 7: Think of a happy, peaceful memory. Give it a name, and write the name here.
_____

Action 8: Continue tapping and rating until both the current and earliest stress memories are at zero.

Action 9: Tap in something that you prefer to experience in place of this stressor. It is usually the opposite of your current and earliest stressor. Give it a name, and write the name here.

_____

Action 10: Check the current and earliest stressors. Are they at zero? If so, great job! If not, continue tapping rounds until they are at zero. In between tapping rounds, be sure to go to your happy, peaceful memory from action 7.

Notes:

_____
_____
_____
_____
_____
_____
_____
_____
_____
_____
_____
_____

CHAPTER 1
Story

● ● ●

The story of "Mary and money" began before I was born, with my parents as depression-era two-year-olds in Milwaukee, living through the crash of 1929. Money beliefs and memories from their parents and the world at large were absorbed into their lives, and subsequently, into mine. This is what we do. We learn from our parents, live their lessons, and pass those lessons on to our kids, however frustrating or unproductive they may be. When something happens, we make the best of it, move on, and work to forget it. The problem is, we never really forget *unless we learn how.*

I was no different—until I learned how to let go of the past with tapping. Technically, the past is over. Moments we have already lived are no longer happening. Before I learned this concept, though, I kept the past alive by ignoring, denying, running, and replaying it, whether consciously or unconsciously.

When I was little, money was often a magical thing. The big people in my life had money, and money made things appear and disappear. When money wasn't magical, it was bad. Like many parents, mine occasionally fought about money, and I learned my beliefs from those stressful moments. Confusion and fear became linked with money, and that became the foundation on which I formed my money habits. I have spent most of my life trying to figure out how to unlink them.

When I was in first grade, we five kids and a couple of neighbors had a band. We set up a stage in our garage and lip-synced to the Beatles or some other hit band that was topping the charts in 1964. Our parents were seated for a concert we gave one weekend, and we told them they could throw money when we were done. They did, and it was one of those magical moments. I felt like a star and believed that all I needed to do was strum a broomstick-guitar, ask for money, and it would be thrown my way forever. I later learned it didn't quite work that way.

Money continued to be a magical notion as I grew, and that perception was echoed by soundbites and movie flashes of *Cinderella*, *Father Knows Best*, *The Jetsons*, and *Underdog*, a cartoon superhero dog. They each took up residence in my young mind and formed beliefs like, "Someday my prince will come and save me from the life of a scullery maid," and "Father works, and mother stays home with the children; she is always dressed to the nines and has dinner on the table at five." I loved the idea of such order in the world. *The Jetsons*, a cartoon television show about a family in the far future, had me hopeful about what was to come. (Much of it has come to pass, with microwaves, Skype and Zoom video conferencing, and treadmills for indoor exercise—but not flying cars; I'm still waiting for those.) I absorbed pieces and parts of these stories and others from childhood, as they reflected my family values and beliefs about my self-worth and about having and making money.

Then, when I was in middle school, everything in our house changed. The family system began to crumble, and all bets were off. While drinking and family parties were normal on holidays and weekends, Dad's drinking and anger escalated. His blackouts and rage became the new norm. We each took cover in our own ways, finding refuge in distractions such as work, school, sports, and darker things like alcohol and drugs. It was a desperate time, and it solidified the resulting post-traumatic stress for me.

Like many of my family members, I used some of those distractions, but I eventually found two abiding ways to disappear: through work and through dissociation.* Work, my external coping mechanism, meant money, and money meant I could escape the war zone of escalating alcoholism. So, I mostly worked.

At first I saved my money, which created a good feeling and a good habit. I felt important, confident, and capable. But as I acquired savings, people I loved would ask me for money, and I complied. It was seldom repaid, but it wasn't their fault; I was the one who had set the ball rolling. I needed them to love me, so I gave whatever they asked for in the hope that they would keep me around for a while longer. This was when another set of beliefs formed: I'm not lovable unless I give people what they want or need, whether they ask for it or not, and it's not my fault when I don't have any money. I didn't know it then, but I was adopting a victim mindset with money, thought habits of poor-me and not-enough-money.

---

* Dissociation is a coping mechanism whereby part of an individual goes to a safe inner place, away from the chaos, while the rest of the person soldiers on.

Underneath these beliefs was the shame core: *I'm not enough. I'm flawed and unlovable.*

My internal coping mechanism as a child was dissociation, and though I was never formally diagnosed with it, the symptoms fit as part of the post-traumatic stress response. I thought everyone else was like me, hypervigilant and anxiously assessing risk and harm moment by moment. The National Alliance of Mental Illness website describes the symptoms of dissociation as:

- significant memory loss of specific times, people, and events.
- out-of-body experiences such as feeling as though you are watching a movie of yourself.
- mental health problems such as depression, anxiety, and thoughts of suicide.
- a sense of detachment from your emotions, or emotional numbness.
- a lack of a sense of self-identity.[2]

With my set of emotional variables and a family system profoundly impacted by alcoholism, my mind and money habits were survival based. I had knowledge gaps about myself and money, and they continued into adulthood. Healthy money habits were a foreign concept.

We lived and survived month by month, year by year. None of us kids learned how to deal with money except by osmosis, observation, and day-to-day experiences. But that was the 1960s; the good news is that some of my siblings nailed their money programs early on and consistently did very well for themselves. I have, too, now, with the help of tapping.

I eventually escaped my home state of Wisconsin and went to college in Florida. I thought a geographic change would offer a solution to my problems, but it didn't. I returned to Wisconsin four months later, freaked out by the reality of what living on my own, all alone, really meant. I didn't like it.

Shortly after I returned, my answer found me: I became a mom. The marriage I found myself in didn't work out, but being a mom did, and motherhood brought with it fierce purpose and determination. At twenty, I was saved from myself by a little babe, and even though I was immature about the ways and means of money (and myself), I knew we would somehow forge a good life. Never mind that the equation of single parenting and saving money would not coexist, especially with my formative beliefs, feelings, and memories. I would figure it out. I would read, research, and find my Underdog way through the complexity of this personal equation. But somewhere inside, I believed money was bad, like me, and probably even a sin. It was confusing but sometimes magical.

My money beliefs played out this way in my mind: *When you have a bit of money saved, you need to give it to those you love so they will love you more and you'll belong. Then you will be broke and back at square one.* I ran this program again and again, trying harder to overcome the invisible habit each time it played, and secretly hoping my Prince Charming would appear to rescue me. I was ill-equipped to make up a story of self-sufficient prosperity for my life and change the thoughts that created my money habits. I kept repeating an invisible, unproductive pattern of not-enough based on the series of beliefs I had, and I didn't know, nor could I have accepted back then, that I was doing it to myself.

The Prince Charming deal didn't work out, but as I said, being a mom did. I became an emotional millionaire three times over; today my kids and their families are daily sources of emotional richness and wealth. Though we were income-restricted through much of their childhood, we laughed, loved, and grew into solid, joyful people of purpose and faith. During my son's seventh birthday party, he suddenly stopped, as we had a moment alone. "Mom, are we poor?" he asked. "Hmm," I said. "We sure don't have a lot of money, do we? But we have a lot of love and fun in our lives. What do you think?" He looked me straight in the eye with the clarity only kids can bring to the table and said, "Nope, we're not poor." Then he ran back out to play with his friends. We made life good no matter what the economic circumstances were.

Still, I knew inside that I could do better for them, model better financial behavior, and be a better provider. Was I doing the best I could with the tools I had? Absolutely. Was I driven to find answers to the money dilemma I had brought from the past? Absolutely. But how do we unadopt an invisible pattern of not-enough? I was so young when those beliefs formed. I knew money was commingled with my notions of self, romantic relationships, PTSD, and a victim mindset. I eventually realized that the missing pieces to the puzzle were to be found in the relationship I had with God and with myself. I had been running from both of us.

In 2006, I stopped running. I asked for help and had an experience with God that spiritually changed me. Things got a lot better after that, but confusion about money and sustaining myself continued. I bought Tony Robbins's "Ultimate Edge" personal development program and did his "Results Coaching" program with one of his trained coaches. After a time, she suggested I get help with the PTSD, as it appeared to be getting in the way of my financial progress. I had tried counseling and talk therapy for years before that, which had acted as a pressure release valve of sorts, but the PTSD triggers had continued despite my best efforts. I kept searching for my own answers.

The chronic PTSD triggers were getting in the way of almost everything, and I was fed up. In 2011, out of desperation, I said a prayer for help to resolve the triggers once and for all. The answer came in the form of the Emotional Freedom Technique (EFT) and FasterEFT/Eutaptics, also known as meridian tapping. This brilliant self-help modality enabled deep change to occur inside my mind and body. Using my fingertips, I tapped on meridian points on my face and started addressing beliefs I held about myself. I learned to tap scary memories from the past that would pop up in the present. I tapped along to hundreds of hours of YouTube videos by Robert G. Smith and others. The videos and Robert's succinct process were profoundly helpful, and I was grateful for the huge benefits I experienced by tapping and watching him tap. Determined to heal and feel better fast, I started tapping daily, and I have continued to do so every day since.

When I combined what I had learned about courage and vulnerability (Brown), tapping (Smith), visioning and success (Canfield), and financial peace (Ramsey), healing and integration started to come together rapidly. I now continue to use tapping to overcome unhealthy and dysfunctional money habits from the past that are rooted in shame, ignorance, and a victim mindset. I had to own, accept, and deconstruct my definition of post-traumatic stress disorder and learn to increase my self-worth.

In rewriting my story, I learned to frame PTSD in different language so that it made sense to me. I owned my part and accepted that I did the best that I could with the tools I had. My current definition of the PTSD I dealt with is this: after bad things happened, I made myself sick by either replaying the scenarios in my head or disappearing and pretending they didn't happen. I don't do that anymore. Now I monitor my thoughts and feelings. If they start heading downward, I take action with tapping.

I'm glad that the past is over and that I didn't give up. I learned to change my thought habits about myself and money, and as a result, I healed. I got better because I stopped making myself sick by replaying bad stories in my mind. That action—taking personal responsibility for the stories I tell myself and others—transformed me. You, too, can identify and change your bad stories so that you can prosper and change the way you live.

Worksheet: Story

Briefly describe the core beliefs you have about yourself.
_____
_____
_____

Briefly outline your current money story.
_____
_____
_____

What are your beliefs about money from childhood?
_____
_____
_____

Do you want to change your money story and the habits that result from your story? _____

How committed are you to changing your mind and money experience? _____
        0 = not at all, 10 = completely committed

What is your current money thermostat setting?
    Not enough
    Just enough
    More than enough
    Plenty

CHAPTER 2

Tapping

Tapping is a tool for life.

In this chapter, we will go deep into step 1, tapping, to see how to it works to crush your obstacles. Tapping utilizes the Chinese acupuncture concept of meridians, or lines, that run along the body and connect points in the hands, feet, arms, and legs to the organs in the body. Doctors of Traditional Chinese Medicine, licensed acupuncturists, place needles in these points to alleviate corresponding physical symptoms. Tapping on certain meridian points on the face applies this same principle, so it can be used as a tool to release stress, remove unproductive patterns, and reduce negative emotions.

The Evolution of the Tapping Movement

Tapping has been around since the 1960s. Here is a timeline of the evolution of tapping up to the current time.

- 1960s: Chiropractor George Goodheart, Jr., starts tapping on meridian points to identify and relieve his patients' pain. It works.
- 1973: Psychiatrist John Diamond, one of Goodheart's students, stimulates meridians with tapping, and his patients get better.
- 1979: Psychologist Roger Callahan, who studied under both Diamond and Goodheart, uses tapping on a client who has a fear of water. Tapping works as a permanent solution to the client's water phobia. As a result, Callahan develops a method of tapping he calls Thought Field Therapy.
- 1987: Patricia Carrington, a student of Callahan's, creates the Acutap method of meridian tapping. It works.
- 1995: Gary Craig, a Stanford-trained engineer and student of Callahan's, creates the Emotional Freedom Technique. It works. (EFT utilizes neurolinguistic programming, an approach to communication, personal development, and psychotherapy created by Richard Bandler and John Grinder in the 1970s.)
- 2004: Robert G. Smith, who studied under Bandler, Craig, and numerous other thought leaders, combines EFT with NLP to develop FasterEFT (recently branded as Eutaptics). This development shows that tapping works quickly with simplified tapping points.
- 2018: Tapping is becoming a mainstream self-help tool for the masses.

Beliefs, Feelings, and Memories

Beliefs, feelings, and memories, or BFMs, are considered to be the trifecta of change, where deep and lasting changes are made.

BELIEFS

Beliefs are formed when we are young, and they continue to develop as we experience life. According to an article published by the National Center for Biotechnology Information, beliefs are negotiable, and we have the power to choose the beliefs we hold: "Beliefs originate from what we hear—and keep on hearing from others, ever since we were children (and even before that!). The sources of beliefs include environment, events, knowledge, past experiences, visualization, etc. One of the biggest misconceptions people often harbor is that belief is a static, intellectual concept. Nothing can be farther from truth! Beliefs are a choice. We have the power to choose our beliefs. Our beliefs become our reality."[3] Tapping is a tool that can help us to choose which beliefs we want to keep and which ones to release.

FEELINGS

We often use the terms *emotion* and *feeling* interchangeably, but according to noted neurologist and author Antonio Damasio, emotion comes first, as a complex neurological reaction to an event; emotion produces physical effects such as sweaty palms, racing heart, tightening muscles, and dry mouth. Damasio says, "Feelings occur after we become aware in our brain of such physical changes; only then do we experience the feeling."[4]

It is interesting to note that with tapping, feelings are technically formed by emotion; however, I personally use the terms "feelings" and "emotions" interchangeably, as they are internal kinesthetic bodily responses to an event (along with the external, physical sensations of touch).

Memories

A memory is the concept of a person, place, thing, or event that is retained, archived, and stored as neural information in the brain for future access. Memories are historic "proof" that something took place. I consider some memories a problem when they are negative and recur unwarranted in the mind. I used to have a habit of mentally avoiding, denying, or being preoccupied with memories from the past because I didn't know what to do with them. I had the same habit pattern with money. I was immature. With tapping, I now have a tool to change negative thoughts and memories, even when I don't fully remember an event.

Change with Tapping

I learned to change intense emotions and memories about not being or having enough by using my index and middle fingers to tap on specific acupressure points. For negative emotional reactions and triggers, tapping proved to be an exacting tool to address BFMs the instant they arose. This built my confidence and felt empowering. Immaturity gave way to curiosity and growth, and I began to find answers to resolving my money issues and the low self-worth I felt.

When we experience a BFM at its strongest intensity, the neural network where it resides is engaged. Tapping interrupts the engaged flow of neurons that are produced by pictures in our heads, movies that we make up, and stories that we see, hear, feel, and rehearse. This interruption process changes the intensity of a BFM and our perception of a feeling or event. Tapping quickly addresses our personal experience of a specific belief, feeling, or memory via the electrical systems of brain and body. Bit by bit, the neurological patterns that are built by our BFMs from the past start to change.

When I first started tapping, I was shocked that it worked. I used to "flood" easily with feelings of low esteem and self-recrimination. I responded poorly to external triggers and struggled with perfectionism. When I was stuck in emotional overwhelm—or worse, flooding (extreme overwhelm coupled with disordered thoughts)—I tapped more often and reached out to FasterEFT practitioners, who mentored me through the tapping change process. Old survival programs were in place back then, so I traded paying the water or electric bill for a session. The bills got paid anyway, and I proved to myself that I was worth investing in. I was diligent. I tapped, studied, and climbed the ranks to practitioner myself, but my economics weren't changing as much or as fast as I wanted.

By tapping on BFMs, my money thermostat moved from not-enough to just-enough, but I wanted it set to more-than-enough and then to plenty. Frustrated, I continued tapping through more BFMs about self and money. Things appreciably changed in 2013 after I attended a tapping session with Robert G. Smith at a "Heal Your Sexual Self" seminar. I felt like I dumped a dozen truckloads of misinformation and old stuff, and this catharsis spurred new habits of thought about myself and money. I addressed the past in the present and thus released my future. Tapping transformed many of my past negative experiences by neutralizing the intense emotions and beliefs I had formed in childhood. The ugly duckling I believed I was started to change, and I didn't even know it.

In 2016, I began reading *The Success Principles* by Jack Canfield. Functionally learning that the past really is over—that it's not a theoretical construct—and taking ownership of the outcomes in my life gave me hope, and I saw traction on releasing the not-enough patterns I had been lugging around since childhood. More money was coming in and therefore more financial self-esteem. I was better able to self-manage emotional information and reduce emotional flooding in the heat of the moment by applying lessons from the many tools I was gathering: scripture, *The Success Principles*, the courage and vulnerability work of Brené Brown, the reticular activating system (RAS), NLP, EFT, and FasterEFT. All of this was great progress for me.

THE SUBJECTIVE UNITS OF DISTRESS SCALE (SUDS)

The Subjective Units of Distress Scale (SUDS)* is a way of quantifying the immediate problem by measuring the intensity of the emotion attached to it. It is particularly helpful for measuring an emotion and then reducing the intensity of the feeling with tapping. Using SUDS, we can clearly identify and rate BFMs by assessing intensity, where 0 = no intensity and 10 = highest intensity. This method is elegant because we can know where we are in the change process. If an issue is at a 10, we can tap until it is 0, thus releasing the problem BFM and the neural structure of the problem at its core.

Having a method to measure stress and then to change it is empowering because what we measure, moves. Couple emo-

---

* For more on SUDS, see "Subjective units of distress scale" at *Wikipedia*: https://en.wikipedia.org/wiki/Subjective_units_of_distress_scale.

tional information with SUDS and tapping, and we have an "intellectual approach to feelings"* jackpot, a do-it-yourself disruptor; disrupt the old emotional patterns of mind and money habits, box them up, and release them from the neural archives forever.

Prosperity is an inside job, and transforming habits on an emotional level is often the most challenging part of this process because feelings are messy. Finding and using a simple structure, like the one I use for tapping, will build your skill in changing unproductive and unhealthy BFMs. As a result of using this structure, your thought habits can change because you learn to process information differently. By tapping in the moment, you are free to let the past go; it isn't real anymore.

I prefer to live right here, right now, in the present. Through my own tapping journey, I have learned to be more mindful of the moment, the only place where real change can happen. When we release BFMs along with other unproductive notions, the emotional path clears. Prosperity, a state of mind where we feel rich in all the things that matter, and with plenty to share, is here. Emotional and financial wealth, once on the distant horizon, is within reach.

Tapping works. I know who lives inside my skin now, and I like this person. She's enough. She is worth the effort and is fun to be with. I accept past money experiences as data points, the necessary learnings that made me into an amazing adventurer, equipped to share a good report of a life well lived. There is no price tag on that one.

The "intellectual approach to feelings" is a term I coined to describe the combination of tapping, data sets, and beliefs, feelings, and memories to intellectually address and release emotion at core levels.

Worksheet: Tapping

What unproductive money habit(s) do you hope to change with tapping?

_____

_____

Write the headline for your first money belief, feeling, or memory (BFM) that you intend to change with tapping.

_____

Rate the intensity of this BFM, where 0 = no stress and 10 = high stress. _____

Using the Quick-Start Guide, tap one round on this issue. Rate it after tapping. What changed?

_____

_____

How do you feel knowing that you can change your BFMs?

_____

_____

Set a date for when you will tap on your unproductive money habits. _____

Name one or two people who can be an accountability partner during your transformation process.

_____

_____

CHAPTER 3
Resolve

● ● ●

Resolve is a resolution or determination made, as to follow some course of action.

In this chapter, we will explore how important step 2, resolve, is to make deep and lasting changes and crush your obstacles. You either have resolve or you don't. You are either the victim or the victor in money pursuits (or anything else).

My formal resolve to crush internal obstacles amalgamated on December 26, 2017, and clarified into this book on March 20, 2018. The idea of crushing the obstacles that stood in my way sprang from a question that my eldest asked me years ago: "Mom, you're so smart. Why is it so hard?" The "it" in question was the economics of life. We were income-restricted for all the years of her childhood. Finances were hard, period. We became *unfortun*ately good (pun intended) at survival, and the money pattern of not-enough took on a life of its own. Her question inspired me to finally find a way to make permanent changes in my mind and financial habits.

Spontaneous Resolve

The resolve to change my money habits appeared spontaneously. I woke up one day and said to myself, *That's it. I've had enough. I choose to live the life of my dreams no matter what it takes. Other people are doing it, and so can I.* Determined to do something "big, hairy, and audacious"—a term Jack Canfield uses in *The Success Principles* (and originally from Jim Collins's book *Built to Last*)—I set a goal of bringing in $365,000 in a year, with time to enjoy it. I resolved that I was even going to beat the goal before a year was up. Why that amount? It represents high self-esteem and value but not so high as to be unattainable.

I decided to make a big, hairy, audacious goal—a BHAG*— and make it SMART: specific, measurable, achievable, results-oriented, and time-bound.*g I learned these two terms while I was working as a manager at an online print shop, and I was reminded about BHAG while reading *The Success Principles*. A SMART goal gets everyone rowing in the same direction at the same time. I needed to get all my thought and money habits moving in the same direction, so making my BHAG a SMART goal helped put structure around a previously unwieldy data set. Data sets are related pieces of information made up of different elements that can be manipulated or moved as a unit. A belief, a memory, and a feeling compose a data set.

---

* BHAG is a term from the book *Built to Last* by Jim Collins and Jerry I. Porras. See Resources for more information.
*George T. Doran, consultant and former director of corporate planning for the Washington Power Company, wrote the SMART acronym in 1981.

My adjusted gross income in 2017 was low in part because I left my job to care for my mom in her final months. I am grateful for the time with her and miss her every day. The choice to serve her during this last season of her life was a solid decision on all levels and formed the basis of my resolve to change my financial mindset. Still, by the end of 2017, my financial thermostat was stuck at just-enough.

To crush this just-enough obstacle, my first step was to find resolve and find it *now*. To me, resolve is a feeling, a knowing, a picture, and a movie: it is the sound I imagine Hulk makes when he's busting a move and his workday clothes have shredded to expose green, rippling muscle. Hulk became my visual anchor. My son made a Hulk painting several years ago, and I look at it daily. When I see it, I'm fired up—even angry sometimes because of past beliefs about myself and the ensuing money habits and behaviors. Each of my data sets around money and myself are now deliberate and proactive. Resolve is the reason I am clear.

Constructed Resolve

If resolve hadn't appeared spontaneously, I would have needed to construct it, because resolve is imperative to crushing obstacles. All the years of searching for answers were probably my "resolve construction period," but if you want to construct resolve, I suggest that you make a list of all the financial don't-wants you have, then read it aloud to really see, feel, and hear them. At the end of the list, say something like, "I've created these outcomes and produced these results. I am changing now." These don't-wants have been driving your unproductive money results unconsciously. I have done this exercise in the past, and it is not a simple mental activity; it must be alive with emotion.

Sitting with don't-wants can be infuriating, but it can also spur resolve. After taking responsibility for your financial results and owning them, your next step is to tap out the unproductive BFMs about money using FasterEFT. The Quick-Start Guide and the instructions in appendix A provide sample BFMs and describe the tapping process.

You *can* find your resolve. You *can* change and transform your mind and money habits. Start with your don't-wants. Identifying the money beliefs you hold in your mind, along with intense feelings that come up in the moment, will point you in the direction of where to tap. Any money memories connected with shame tend to be intense because they are about you and your self-perception. The stronger you can feel your displeasure, the faster resolve comes and the faster the BFM releases with tapping.

If reading your list of don't-wants ever produces the opposite of resolve (fear, weakness, indecision, wavering, etc.), you have a choice to make. You can either keep the fear and continue to produce mediocre financial results, or you can let the fear and wavering go, embrace the suck, and wade through the thought habits that work against you. It may not always feel like it, but resolve is a choice. Without resolve, consistent forward progress on a negative money pattern is elusive.

Until I said "Enough!" my results were inconsistent. I needed resolve to get through obstacle crushing; it drives the BHAG. When I am in a lull and not sure what to do, I go right back to that moment when I said "*Enough*, this pattern is done." Then I see the amount of $365,000 in my mind, the

Hulk, my kids, and my grandkids, and I take the next indicated right action in front of me.

> After you find resolve, whether spontaneous or constructed, find a picture that represents it. Use a visual that really fires you up, something that moves you to act with resolve on your personal BHAG. Makes copies, and put them everywhere.

Worksheet: Resolve

"I am 100 percent resolved to change my money habits." On a scale of 0 to 100, how true is this statement for you today?

What kind of resolve do you have?

- spontaneous resolve
- constructed resolve

List your financial and money don't-wants. (If you need more space, there are additional pages at the back of the book.)

_____

_____

How are these don't-wants showing up in your life today?

_____

_____

What are your do-wants with finances and money?

_____

_____

What pictures are you using to represent resolve?

_____

_____

CHAPTER 4

Own

To own is to acknowledge as belonging to one; to recognize as having full claim, authority, power, and dominion of something.

In this chapter, you will learn how step 3, owning the results in your life, is vital to crushing obstacles. Owning the results of my choices was tough for me. The obstacles to prosperity, or anything else I wanted in life—including high self-esteem—were self-initiated stories based on the past. To crush obstacles and transform money habits with tapping, I had to own my current results, which felt bad. Owning these results meant I had to take responsibility for their creation. Canfield's *The Success Principles* presses the point home that we are 100 percent responsible for the outcomes in our lives. As I was reading the book, I finally *got it*. There was no more running from the results I had created.

When I first started reading *The Success Principles* in mid-2016, I didn't get all the way through it. I ended up putting the book down, got stuck in a shame spiral, and couldn't find my way out. In 2017, I picked up the book again, but now I had to own the fact that I had put it down unfinished. I had to own my current financial results (including the lack of follow-through), and I had to own the fact that I still felt bad about myself. I decided to recommit. I was curious to see where I had stopped reading. I saw that I had wavered at "Decide What You Want," and then I quit altogether at "Believe It's Possible."

Owning the outcomes in my life was unpleasant at first. I had built an identity around not-having-enough and not-being-enough in the finance department. In my mind, I had given myself props for working so hard and having so little to show for it. I'm sure there were other aspects to this pattern, otherwise I wouldn't have practiced my not-enough program for so long.

Own Your Money Pattern

The unproductive money pattern I used to run in my mind and in my life was built on a victim mindset: *Poor me; I don't know how to change my money pattern; I'm a single parent who received little child support. I'm not smart enough or good enough, and I'm bad at math.* Neurologically, this money pattern was an unconscious network of beliefs, feelings, and memories that consistently produced less than what I needed.

I avoided owning my results because I didn't have a filter on my past experiences. I didn't know what to do with the past. I had heard the phrase "the past is over" many times and knew on a cognitive level that yesterday is done and tomorrow isn't here yet, but the emotional past wasn't over on a gut level. No one had taught me emotional self-discipline.

In order to move beyond this stage, I had to take new steps to own and change my BFMs and then consciously dial the money thermostat up to more-than-enough and plenty. In *The Success Principles*, Canfield suggests taking five actions every day that move us toward our goals. Here are five steps I took:

1. Notice where I am financially: not-enough, just enough, more than enough, or plenty. What are my current beliefs?
2. Notice what I want.
3. Make a choice. Decide what I prefer for the future.
4. Take action.
5. Find a protocol that will help me reach my goal. (I used FasterEFT/Eutaptics to help myself emotionally release old thought patterns and establish new ones, and Financial Peace University to physically establish new money habits.)

Here is an example of my thought process and how I took some steps:

> Today I feel scared about investing in myself to get this book into the hands of librarians, avid book lovers, and the media. I can attend the National Publicity Summit, but I am afraid to invest real money into the process. My fears come from past failures and thoughts of unworthiness . . . wait! That's a clue! Do I want to keep those BFMs or let them go? I want to

let them go. I tap out my old BFMs around investing in myself.

I apply to the National Publicity Summit and am accepted. I purchase Amy Collins's "Library Profit System" to learn how to get this book into libraries across the country. I have now changed my mind about investing in myself.

Taking five actions each day to achieve success is not only an excellent practice, but the daily actions become momentum that inspires and guides our next steps.

Reframe

Reframing our emotional data sets takes discipline. To let go of the emotional past, I developed skill in managing emotion as a data set, a specific series of beliefs, feelings, and memories that are triggered by an internal or external event. For the internal data set I have frequently dealt with of not-enough-money, I held the *belief* that there wasn't enough money and that there wouldn't ever be enough. The *feelings* were helplessness and hopelessness, and the *memory* was me as a second-grader standing in the kitchen listening to my parents talk about not-enough-money.

I started noticing the data set of not-enough-money when it came up in real time. For example, when I kept checking my bank balance to see if a payment had arrived, I would recognize that behavior as being based on the not-enough-money data set. I acknowledged it, and reminded myself that the past is over and that I am no longer in second grade. When I would recognize the behavior, my internal monologue would go something like this: *Not enough money was a data set inside me. It was unproductive, and I choose to let it go.* Then I would take action to let it go with tapping. This is how I reframed that money belief. Over time, I learned that feelings aren't facts; they are simply one of the ways we process information, and they can change from moment to moment. I also learned that beliefs and memories can be changed.

The emotional skill of reframing BFMs as data sets is empowering and critical to the process of crushing obstacles and transforming our mind and money habits. Instead of experiencing a trigger and swirling around in unidentified BFMs with no way out and no way to resolve the conflict, you can realize that you have the skill to make a choice. You can ask yourself questions to help you reframe your thinking (I still do). You can learn to objectify your emotional experience with questions like these and then to make different choices:

- Do you want to keep this BFM or let it go?
- When was the last time you felt this feeling?
- When was the first time you felt it?
- What do you believe because of this BFM?
- Are you sure you want to let it go? Do you gain something by keeping this belief?
- What might happen if you let it go?

Having a mental checklist like this helped me to convert an experience, memory, feeling, or belief into a data set. Once I named the problem with a short title, it became easier to process and release. My emotional habits were changing!

As I tapped out unproductive emotional responses to triggers, I found that my feelings and memories were easier to deal with. I realized that my identity and self-concept could be distinctly separate from my kinesthetic responses. I hadn't known it was possible to separate myself from my emotional responses, and being able to do so was revolutionary. Perhaps most people learn this concept through the process of maturation, but I missed it.

Reframing emotional information into a data set (akin to a Word doc in a folder on my computer) created a remarkable shift in me. Instead of flooding—the act of creating and keeping overwhelming beliefs, feelings, and memories "flooding" to the surface—when I was triggered by shame or another intense (and often unproductive) emotion, I was able to step back, review the belief, feeling, or memory at play, and cognitively box it up. This reframing process yielded a clean, objective information set that responded to tapping.

Once I learned to repackage BFMs in this way, the trigger, whatever it was, lost its power. I would (and sometimes still do) picture Data, the character from *Star Trek: The Next Generation*, as an internal resource to help me. Now when I imagine how Data might address a belief, feeling, or memory about me or money, I laugh because he would probably say, "Beliefs, feelings, and memories are not facts, and therefore they are not real, Mary." That makes sense to me!

I now regularly practice detaching from emotion and review each emotion as a data set. As a result, I have an intellectual approach to feelings that increases my capacity to be mindful and present in the moment. Being present is the opposite of dissociating, and I need to be present in order to change my mind and habits. The protective coping skill from childhood, where I learned to cut and run somewhere inside myself to be safe, no longer serves me. I am safe now. I'm a grown-up. I can and do self-manage emotional information without overloading by boxing it up as an information data set and then tapping.

Own Your Emotions and Set Boundaries for BFMs

I used to be good at flooding—keeping myself emotionally overwhelmed—which led to a host of unproductive responses. I would feel helpless, an old feeling from childhood, and would seem to become hypnotized by the past. I still thought the BFMs were real. This was not an optimal state because continually reprocessing old stuff only reinforces the neural networks on which they were built. It's like lifting weights: when you work a specific group of muscles, they grow stronger. This unproductive pattern of flooding reinforced overwhelm, inaction, and a sustained feeling of helplessness.

Now that I take personal responsibility for my outcomes, successes, and failures, I reframe them as needed and experience a freedom I didn't have before. I still remember and process traumatic pieces of the past from time to time. I don't ignore or deny them, but I put a boundary in place to make those pieces manageable. For me, that boundary includes taking time to observe the BFMs at hand so that I can transform them into simple data sets.

To help me keep this boundary, I created a picture in my mind of a very large wooden door. This is a special door, as it holds the past in its place. My door is guarded by a huge, muscular angel, and nothing flows out of the door unless I request it—nothing. I believe that we never have more than we can handle in the moment, including emotions, and this door is part of what makes my life manageable.

In order to make this visualization a usable resource in my mental world, I had to shift from a cognitive understanding that the past is over to a visceral, emotional understanding. I had wondered how that intellectual shift would happen, and for me, it was with tapping. I boxed up latent emotional stuff from the past and released it from my mind. It took a while.

Now that my door to the past is constructed, I practice using it every day. If I want, I can hear it close and lock *click*—and it's done. I take a deep breath and imagine the feeling of relaxation, that just-had-a-massage-and-all-is-well-in-the-world kind of feeling. The past is in its place. Relief pours over me. This is my preferred present,* and the past is now manageable. I function more effectively knowing that the door to my past is sealed off. If I need to process a piece of information, I imagine going up to the door, saying hello to the angel guarding it, and verifying my identity. Since I am the one making up this little movie, I also created another aspect: a computer keyboard and a high-tech eye scanner for identity verification. Only I can obtain the info I need; no one else has access to it.

Knowing that all that past stuff is locked behind the door is a huge relief. Before this boundary was in place, I would experience a trigger in my outer world and then be flooded by past BFMs. I would swirl with too much data at a time and have to shut down. It was like having too many appliances on one electrical circuit, causing the breaker to blow and the lights to go out. When this occurred, I would be an emotional mess. In the beginning of my tapping career and changing habits of mind, this flooding happened often, and I didn't understand

---

*"Preferred present" is a term I coined to describe a lovely dream that happens while we are awake. It is a constructed series of pictures, movies, feelings, sensations, and sounds that feed the reticular activating system (RAS) until the desired outcome is achieved.

what was going on. I sought coaching assistance and worked with a fine tapping pro, Edie Carver, for a year and a half. Then I progressively learned to self-manage emotional states, and now I help others do the same.

I don't blow up my emotional fuse box anymore. With resolve, I can stay on task. If I become flooded with too much data (BFMs), I own it and consciously close the door to the past. Then I focus on the *one* belief, the *one* feeling, or the *one* memory that is causing turbulence, one data set at a time, and I tap on that feeling.

What does the past have to do with transforming mind and money habits? Since our financial results are dictated by our BFMs from the past, we have to get a handle on what is going on inside us in order to change the outcomes. We have to accept that we hold these beliefs. Perhaps you hold beliefs like, "It'll never happen; I can't; I'm not good enough; I'm not smart enough; it's all my fault; I deserve to be punished; money is bad; money is a sin; you should give it all away," and so on. Once we reframe these beliefs as objective data sets instead of a shameful identity, we can understand that we are responsible for producing our current financial outcomes. Then we can take each belief, one by one, rate it with SUDS, and tap each one down to 0.

All these changes took a while for me, and it takes discipline to stay with the process. First, we must take responsibility for the belief, then own it, tap it, and ultimately change it to an opposite, prosperous belief. I proved to myself that I could change my BFMs by making them into data sets that transformed with tapping. This gave me courage to tackle the victim-and-money mindset, which led to building my confidence and self-esteem.

Worksheet: Own

I am 100 percent responsible for the financial results I currently have in my life.

                True   False

The past is over.

                True   False

I know the past is over, but it doesn't *feel* like it's over.

                True   False

What does flooding look and feel like to you?

_____

_____

How has flooding impacted your finances?

_____

_____

What action steps can you take today that will identify and release unproductive data sets that come up in your life?

_____

_____

How do you deal with unresolved issues from the past?

_____

_____

How is that approach working for you?

CHAPTER 5
VAKOG

VAKOG is an acronym for the senses: visual, auditory, kinesthetic, olfactory, and gustatory.

In this chapter, we will dig into step 4, exploring and learning how to create positive, productive beliefs, feelings, and memories using clean VAKOG. The acronym "VAKOG" is an NLP term coined by Richard Bandler and John Grinder and refers to information processing—*how* we represent our lives, loves, and experiences. It stands for visual (pictures), auditory (sounds), kinesthetic (feelings and touch), olfactory (smells), and gustatory (taste) information. Our VAKOG informs our opinions and creates our perceptions, which in turn create our thoughts and actions, which then produce results. VAKOG is critical when it comes to any thought habits we have, especially about self-esteem and money. It is also a critical component of the PTSD experience.

When I read Bob Bodenhamer and Michael Hall's book *The User's Manual for the Brain* while I was doing the *Ultimate Learning Kit* from the Skills to Change Institute, I learned that everybody makes pictures, movies, soundtracks, feelings, sensations, smells, and tastes when they experience something. As the authors explain, "In the NLP model, the five senses do far more than just funnel information. Each system receives information and then activates memories to produce behavior."[5]

These five senses activate our memories. For me, once a memory is activated, I go into the process of being triggered, positively or negatively. When the reaction is negative, I am unresourceful, and when it is positive, I'm unstoppable, able, and creative. This is where the true action in crushing old money habits and mental obstacles happens. When we are in a state of auto-response, which some call a trance, we are in a state of acute inward attention. We are neurologically "tasking" on a trigger and don't even know it.

Many of us are not aware that we play pictures, movies, sounds, feelings, sensations, smells, and tastes in our heads whenever we do something, especially things that have to do with money. We tend to run on default settings that simply and consistently produce sub-par money results. Even when we want to change the default setting, we don't know how. What are the steps to creating mediocre financial results? Once we have the recipe, we can change it.

I realized that many of my beliefs formed "packets" of negative feelings and audio (the "auditory" in VAKOG) in the form of internal monologue. As a little girl, I was hypersensitive to the tone of voice and words people used to communicate with me. Eventually I internalized those negative audio files, especially the ones that were repeatedly delivered with anger or shame. That early information became my self-talk. For years I didn't know I was producing negative self-talk that, in turn, was producing negative feelings and pictures. The audio was running in the background of my mind 24/7, unconsciously initiating negative emotional reactions.

    I figured this out one day when a friend called me for support and then began whining—something for which I have a low tolerance. I felt irritated, helpless, and angry. I was in the midst of writing this book and knew I was 100 percent responsible for my responses, so I asked myself what this friend might be mirroring in *my* life. Where was I whining, helpless, and irritated?

    I took the time to really scan myself for whining. I realized that I don't whine when I communicate with others, but I do whine in my thoughts to myself. When I realized this pattern, I decided to unravel the process and change what I say to myself about myself and anyone else. My scan also revealed a whining data point on my timeline. My dad used to come unglued when any of us five kids whined. No specific memories pop into place, but the thought of whining as a kid still makes me flinch, so there must have been some forceful persuasion involved. I have since tapped that out. The belief from that time is, "No one is allowed to whine. If someone whines, they are bad and will be made to stop." The data set is extreme agitation, simultaneous fight-flight-and-freeze feelings, and the feeling of wanting to jump out of my skin. The memory? Nothing specific. It is simply a knowing that whining was verboten.

    This kind of assessment takes practice, presence of mind, and self-awareness. To transform my money mindset, I knew

I had to *crush* whining, that negative internal monologue that is present when I am idling between activities. This idling space was my downfall. What was I doing in my head when I wasn't actively engaged in an activity? I was talking to myself with words that were unkind, unsupportive, or discouraging about something from the past or coming up in the future. NLP defines information projected into the future as "future pacing."* Once I noticed that I routinely engaged in unproductive idling activity, I was able to interrupt that pattern with tapping and redirect my focus to the present. This became an important part of my process to crush obstacles and transform.

Here are some of idling activities I used to do frequently:

- Prepare for a conversation or event (unconscious future pacing**)
- Review a past conversation or event (unconscious recycling***)
- Process miscellaneous thoughts unattached to any specific desired outcome
- Be mindful or quiet (as in meditation), remembering the meditative state
- Pray for special intentions for myself and others
- Worry, or an unconscious recycling loop of mental activity that made me feel like I was doing something about a situation over which I had no control.

---

* For more information on future pacing, see "Methods of neuro-linguistic programming" at *Wikipedia*, https://en.wikipedia.org/wiki/Methods_of_neuro-linguistic_programming.

** "Unconscious future pacing" is a term I coined to identify what I was doing in my mind so I could name it and change it quickly. It means unknowingly projecting thoughts, often negative, into the future.

*** "Unconscious recycling" is a term I coined. It means unknowingly processing and reprocessing events and memories experienced in the past.

Polluted VAKOG

Polluted VAKOG* are negative pictures, movies, sounds, feelings, sensations, smells, and tastes that we reproduce in our minds and bodies based on negative events of the past. These are what I had used to create low self-esteem and the consistently mediocre financial outcomes I experienced. Without realizing it, I had fed my mind with these negative soundtracks, feelings, sensations, and bad movies: pollution about myself, my abilities, and the world.

Memories are experiences of the past, both good and bad. I had unconsciously learned to refer to bad memories because they were emotionally charged and therefore more anchored in my recollection. I didn't want to experience those negative things again, so for years I focused heavily on them just to make sure they didn't recur. I practiced this unconscious habit particularly about money and romantic relationships. Focusing on what we are afraid of (to guard against it) seems counterintuitive, but I think unconscious recycling is a common practice. I now recognize this as a processing error and realize that a hyper-focus on the negative is precisely how I created negative financial and relationship outcomes.

My previous mindset was created by polluted VAKOG: *I'm no good. I'm not loveable. Financial increase will never happen for me. Things will never change. It's too late. I feel hopeless, helpless, angry, and resentful of others who seem to have everything.* This negative data set controlled me and my financial outcomes, and I was unconsciously doing it to myself. I didn't know how to stop until I accepted 100 percent responsibility

---

* "Polluted VAKOG" is a term I coined to describe negative thinking made of fearful, scary, and unproductive pictures, movies, soundtracks, feelings, smells, and tastes.

for my life. Then I followed the information trail and asked, *How on earth did I consistently produce experiences of not-enough in money, self-esteem, and love?*

Don't ask why, ask *how*: how do I consistently produce negative outcomes? I did it with low self-worth and negative beliefs, feelings, and memories of myself from the past and years of practice.

Now that I am consciously changing my habits and cleaning up my thoughts, positive results are flowing into my life. I am grateful for the phone call trigger that led to my awareness of whining and polluted VAKOG. I simply hadn't realized my negative thinking patterns were producing my belief in not-enough and that my BFMs were hurting me, my finances, and ultimately, my children. I take my parenting responsibilities to heart, so knowing that I have modeled how to produce inferior financial results with polluted VAKOG is distressing at best. I continue to tap on those BFMs when they arise and reframe this long-term challenge in the moment. It is an opportunity to change myself and teach others how to change, too.

Perhaps one day soon, we will all know and understand how we process information. Armed with this fundamental and critical awareness, we can amend habits that foster polluted VAKOG. Instead of running on unconscious defaults, we can teach that beliefs, feelings, and our perceptions of memories can and do change with intentional effort. Polluted VAKOG leaves clues. Listening closely to the words people use tells me whether they are primarily visual, auditory, or kinesthetic (feeling/sensation-based). When I am present and aware, I tailor my communication to build rapport with others based on this information. I also listen closely to what

I say about myself and others, and change my words when necessary. Polluted VAKOG can easily be in the form of judgment, criticism, or gossip, so I have learned to stop negative talk or to physically disengage from conversations that are predominantly polluted by leaving the room.

Clean VAKOG

The term "clean VAKOG"* came about while I was trying to better my self-talk. It describes powerful, resourceful pictures and movies that support, encourage, and inspire us. Clean VAKOG are positive, encouraging scripts that we can create and recite or read to ourselves to replace the old, negative thoughts that we are used to thinking. I have learned to inspire, coach, and encourage myself by creating affirming monologues, pictures, and movies that make me feel good. I can imagine a movie in which I believe in myself and have all the support and money I need in my life. This sounds a little kumbaya, but the fact is, unless we change our mindset, nothing else will change. The way I have learned to change my mind is to mentally produce clean VAKOG. That said, changing from polluted VAKOG to clean takes work.

Good pictures, movies, soundtracks, feelings, and sensations decrease the stress response, and the mind and body can relax. Using clean VAKOG, we have more resources to feel strong and competent, and are able to put our thoughts aside and listen to others. An important thing to note is that clean VAKOG becomes food with which to feed a part of the brain called the "reticular activating system," or RAS (more on this

---

* "Clean VAKOG" is a term I coined to describe positive, resourceful thinking made of happy, safe, supportive, and kind pictures, movies, soundtracks, smells, and tastes.

in the next chapter), a part of the brain that filters and sorts important information. When we are relaxed, calm, happy, and peaceful, our bodies know it.

The old internal monologues, pictures, and feelings were the very things that created not-enough in all departments of my life, including money. With polluted VAKOG, my pulse increased, my breathing shallowed, and my cortisol levels rose, taxing the adrenals. The adrenal glands get tired when they are under stress; they work too hard and produce too much cortisol. We need cortisol when we are in a fight-or-flight situation, such as running from a rhinoceros, but we don't need it to fix dinner for our family or get ready for work in the morning.

When we produce clean VAKOG, everything settles down and our stress response is deactivated. Our bodies know that the only time to stop the stress reaction is when threats are eliminated and we are again safe and secure. Breathing becomes deep and unhurried, pulse is steady, and we feel peace. This was a rare occurrence for me when I was experiencing PTSD.

VAKOG Habits

My polluted VAKOG habits had created a bad cycle that engaged both my brain and my body in unhealthy ways. With all I needed to work on, I had to learn how to begin crushing these negative habits and mental obstacles in order to run clean VAKOG. Here are a few of the small, consistent actions I took:

- I learned to change what I do with idling time. If we always do what we have always done, we will always get what we have always gotten. I had to review hour by hour what I was doing with my mindspace. I learned to identify which VAKOG system was involved (visual, auditory, kinesthetic, olfactory, or gustatory), then I discarded the polluted beliefs, movies, feelings, sensations, and sounds with tapping. The *moment* something stressful happened, I ran clean VAKOG. This method works for me, but of course you are free to find your own way.

- I scripted kind, encouraging, and supportive monologues to replace the previous internal monologues. I consciously run new, positive audio scripts when I am between thought activities.
- I created a vision board with positive pictures and feelings to review and experience numerous times daily. A key is to see them as if they have already happened.
- I established a daily habit of meditation and prayer.
- I began a daily practice of FasterEFT-style tapping and a focus on clean VAKOG.
- I began to listen to music that inspires me, such as Katy Perry's "Fireworks," Bobby McFerrin's "Don't Worry, Be Happy," and ocean sounds with whales and dolphins. I listen to music often and fill up on clean auditory inputs. Violins are particularly soothing, so when I do paperwork, I play violin music in the background, which reminds me that all is well and I am at ease.
- I use my phone to keep pictures, movies, and positive self-talk recordings immediately accessible for idling times.
- I go outside for a run, walk, or hike in nature.

- I idle with gratitude. I run through a quick list of ten to twenty things I'm grateful for *right now*, reciting them either aloud or in my head.

I am learning and practicing "image cycling," a process developed by researcher, educator, and author William Bengston (see Resources). I write down twenty-five things I want, and then create a data set for each item based on pictures, sounds, feelings, sensations, smells, and tastes. Numerous times a day I very quickly run all twenty-five data sets in my mind, like a movie. This instills clean VAKOG throughout the day.

The process of changing habits of mind and running clean VAKOG may sound simple, but it takes focus and practice when you are first learning it. A daily routine of thirty-minute meditations is accelerating my ability to observe my thoughts, be still, and access peace inside. The stillness allows me to note what is going on in my head so I can clean up the VAKOG. I didn't start with thirty minutes, I started with five, as that was all I could manage at first. Meditation has become a practice I can't live without, because I want that quiet calm with me all through the day.

A new self-care activity I practice is taking breaks throughout the day to listen to a brief meditation or review my vision board. This helps me detach, observe, breathe, and imagine my new life as it quickly approaches. I take a deep breath and "live into"* clean VAKOG. Sometimes I visualize a favorite beach in Fiji or my home in Carmel, smelling the salty air and hearing the squeaking sand underfoot even as I walk the

---

* "Live into" is a term I use to describe conscious future pacing. It is how I imagine in real time that my happy pictures, movies, sounds, experiences, and positive beliefs are happening right this minute.

corridors at work. Using image cycling, I consciously run a script with rich, clean VAKOG that "all is well." This practice is quickly changing not only my financial results but the very essence of my identity for the better. I am happy, satisfied, and more contented in the moment.

When I am triggered, I work quickly to identify the polluted VAKOG and adjust my thoughts. I tell myself, *This trigger is from the past. It's temporary. This moment was created by past thought. The past is over. I am changing my mind right now. Life is outrageous and fun. I love to help others and serve. Thank you, God.* I also ask myself, *Do you want to keep this trigger or let it go, Mary?* Then I change my mind in the moment and run a clean VAKOG script I previously created for myself. If I am at home or in a situation where I can stop my activities, I literally stop what I'm doing and run my clean VAKOG. I don't wait until later, I do it right there, in the moment.

Here is an example: I'm driving my car, and I notice polluted VAKOG—an angry, sad, or scared reaction to an event. I pause, take a deep breath, notice the pollution, and make a choice to play clean VAKOG in my mind. I run a happy, calm, and safe little movie about what a great day it is, and I feel thankful. This clean VAKOG can be spontaneous or it can be a previously created audio or movie script that I say out loud while I picture myself having achieved all the items on my vision board. I may do a fake laugh* or sing a song, which leads to real laughing out loud and a sudden shift in VAKOG from polluted to clean.

If the trigger has lingered and I'm stuck for more than a few minutes, I tap. If the trigger takes over and I find myself

---

* Fake laughing interrupts polluted VAKOG. I learned and practiced it at seminars conducted by Robert G. Smith.

unresourceful (angry, sad, hurt, resentful, etc.) for longer than an hour, I get help. I reach out to others (such as other FasterEFT and mind-body practitioners) who believe and know on an emotional level that the past is over. These are people who understand that polluted thoughts pollute the day and that a trigger is simply a trigger, a piece of information from the past coming to the surface for release and healing.

It helps a lot to have clear, grounded, supportive people in my life, but I have had to cultivate these relationships with intention. I have also had to become a friend to myself. For example, I'm in the parking lot after finishing shopping, but I forgot to buy my favorite yerba mate sparkling drink. I don't feel like running back into the store because it's cold outside. Then something shifts inside, and I say aloud or in my head, "I'll go get it for you, you're important! I want you to be happy!" That is my new, clean VAKOG. I'm still shocked when I hear positive internal monologue like this; it is kind and helpful, like something I would say to a friend or family member. But I want to be clear: although this sounds easy, in the early stages of acquiring clean VAKOG skills, it is work.

VAKOG Discipline

It took discipline and practice for me to switch from polluted to clean VAKOG. I was so bombarded with negative pictures, sounds, feelings, and sensations from inside and out that forming this new habit wasn't easy. When I would forget that change is an inside job or if I wasn't clear that I am 100 percent responsible for myself, I would easily cave in to the stimuli and become part of the problem.

Discipline is at the root of change. Now I know that there are two distinct options for my thoughts—clean or polluted

VAKOG—and I understand that the one that is happening is my choice. Do I choose generous, kind thoughts, pictures, movies, feelings, and sensations or fearful pictures and sounds that clank around like pots and pans between my ears? Do I listen to inner stories of hope, encouragement, and faith in the greater good or a jumble of thoughts, doubt, and free-floating worry in a sea of mental debris?

We don't need to repeat the negative sights, sounds, feelings, and sensations we experienced while growing up, but we can (and should) keep the good ones. It is up to us to change and to imagine differently for ourselves. I have proven to myself that by choosing new VAKOG in the moment, these resourceful pictures, movies, soundtracks, and feelings are changing my life and my finances forever.

An example of the benefit of running clean VAKOG came up the other day at dinner with my son and his family. We were discussing the names that five-year-old Emmie likes to be called: Dear, Honey, Sweetie, Sweetest, and Sis. Out of my mental archives, I remembered and shared that my dad used to call me Skeezicks and that it made me feel very loved. My son had never heard this story. He paused, taking in a new picture of the grandfather he barely knew. Clean VAKOG is a gift.

With discipline, we can learn to flip a switch inside our brains from beliefs that say, "I'm an unlovable failure" to beliefs that say "I am loved. I'm cherished. I know I can do whatever I set my mind to do. I am thankful for today. Life is good."

I have fun and laugh each day because I understand I am responsible for all my experiences with myself and others. With VAKOG discipline, I amplify the good and feel myself growing. Tapping and grace have healed the wounded child parts that longed for attention and comfort. Perhaps this is a new level of adulting! I am relieved to finally be free from a scary past that I was unknowingly recreating in my thoughts. I feel comfortable and safe being me. Having never before formed a sentence with these particular thoughts and words, I know this is an enormous shift. It is internal prosperity, and on the outside, I have plenty of money, too. I am crushing it! I am transforming my money habits and mindset with tapping.

The new scripts we write for ourselves can be based on gratitude. They can feed our mind's information filter with experiences of joy and abundance. Some of my favorites are, *You're doing great! I appreciate your hard work. I believe in you! Thank you for being you! I'm so proud of you. You look pretty today. You've turned into such a fine woman* (in my dad's voice). Understanding VAKOG empowers us to let go of the past and express grateful, clean VAKOG, which in turn can produce prosperity in ways we never imagined possible.

> I would maintain that thanks are the highest form of thought, and that gratitude is happiness doubled by wonder.
> —GK CHESTERTON

Worksheet: VAKOG

Think about a time in the past when you learned a new skill such as riding a bicycle or driving a car. Did you make up pictures, movies, and sounds, or do you just have a general knowing or sensation in creating that memory?

_____
_____
_____

How do you produce polluted VAKOG?

_____
_____
_____

What kinds of VAKOG do those closest to you produce?

_____
_____
_____

What can you do to produce clean VAKOG?

_____
_____
_____

How do you quiet your mind?

_____

_____

What are your particular idling habits?

_____

_____

_____

What idling habits would you prefer to have?

_____

_____

_____

CHAPTER 6
RAS
◈ ◈ ◈

The reticular activating system, or RAS, is the gatekeeper of the mind.

This chapter discusses step 5, how to apply the brain's reticular activating system (RAS) to filter the information that we let into our minds. When I found out about the RAS and put it to a specific use, I learned to see myself and my thought habits differently and make new choices. Armed with awareness, tapping, and this information, I am changing. I am making emotional and financial gains and fast becoming the woman of my dreams.

The RAS is a part of the brain that sorts and filters information into bite-sized bits so that the important stuff gets through. Psychologist Sharon Linde describes the RAS like this:

> The reticular activating system, or RAS, is a piece of the brain that starts close to the top of the spinal

column and extends upwards around two inches. It has a diameter slightly larger than a pencil. All your senses (except smell, which goes to our brain's emotional center) are wired directly to this bundle of neurons that's about the size of your little finger. Often, the RAS is compared to a filter or a nightclub bouncer that works for your brain. It makes sure your brain doesn't have to deal with more information than it can handle. Thus, the reticular activating system plays a big role in the sensory information you perceive daily.[6]

All data sets, beliefs, feelings, and memories from the past inform the RAS, which filters out things that aren't important and filters in things that are. If low self-esteem and financial don't-wants run the show, we are feeding our RAS polluted VAKOG, which will then bring the don't-wants right to us. When we consciously feed our RAS rich details of a BHAG (that big, hairy, audacious goal!) as if it were completed, we feel great and are constructively participating in the process of its creation.

See It, Hear It, Feel It, and Be It

> Start where you are.
> Dwell on the good in your life.
> —CANDI PARKER, *SHIFT HAPPENS*

No matter what, I am committed to doing the necessary work to be open to new information and to mentally create situations that bring about prosperity. For me, the work consists of living in the present, staying present, and then, every hour or two, "tricking" my mind with clean VAKOG and ignoring the pollution. When I can't ignore the pollution and I am triggered, I notice it and then tap on the negative memory that is consuming my attention. This takes practice.

I grew up in an alcoholic home, and it felt like all my family members were issued a stun gun and a taser to use during confusing or scary events. The image I have of my RAS is a bouncer standing at the door of my mind, with a taser on one hip and a stun gun on the other.

I have learned to zap the pollution in my mind and quickly stow it away in the deep freeze—in my unconscious mind—so I can function. The difference between the unconscious mind and subconscious mind is made clear by PsycholoGenie, an online resource that breaks down psychology concepts for the ordinary human: "When you ask someone to recall the most painful event of their life, he/she may be able to invoke some memories of it from their subconscious mind, but not entirely. Some of the most painful memories linked with that event are subdued forcefully by a part of human mind. This is unconscious mind."[7]

"Subdued forcefully." I like that. This is my RAS at work. To me, the subconscious mind is like a freezer compartment on a fridge, and the unconscious mind is a commercial blast freezer. The unconscious mind brings down the temperature of the emotion and memory fast, for long-term storage. My bouncer-RAS zaps the memory, pushes the "go" button, and quickly freezes and stows the memory in my unconscious mind.

In my estimation, the RAS was conditioned to respond to life events according to a pre-programmed response. For a long time, I didn't know how that programming happened or how to change it. My mental bouncer, objective and impersonal, filtered information based on early childhood experiences of fear, scarcity, helplessness, and low esteem. This fundamentally affected my money habits. I looked for a switch to flip on my RAS so that I could turn off early settings and reprogram it to filter new and positive information. I didn't find a switch, but I learned to change my RAS with clean VAKOG and tapping.

I am relational in nature and need to connect in order to understand concepts more fully, so I built a relationship with my RAS and got to know it. I now picture a male bodyguard/bouncer-type character who silently protects and serves me. I imagined uploading a new job description to him, one that consists of clean VAKOG to keep me safe, protected, loved, and prosperous. I review the clean VAKOG that I feed my RAS daily, and I work to keep my mind clear of debris and pollution.

When we feed our RAS pictures of gratitude and abundance, soundtracks of affirmation, and feelings of certainty and hope, the material results change quickly. How quickly they change depends on us; when we are triggered negatively, it is easy to slip, lightning fast, into polluted mental defaults. This is a learned behavior, an unproductive habit from childhood. When it happens, our RAS takes the polluted VAKOG, filters it, and *voilà*, stress appears in the mind, body, or finances. We may experience racing thoughts, tight shoulders, increased pulse, and so on.

One time, while I was in this state, I noticed a pattern of thought that was keeping me stuck. It was an internal monologue that was repeatedly asking, *How can I change this?* The monologue continued with, *I don't know how, I don't know what to do.* It sounded like a little kid who didn't know what to do in a grown-up world. I tapped on this specific internal monologue, and it changed. Now, when I catch myself wondering, *How am I going to resolve this* or *How will that happen*, I stop myself. These thoughts are signs that I have slipped into an old pattern of distrust and am feeding my RAS polluted VAKOG.

A True Story

My car runs on gasoline. It runs well for four hundred miles on clean fuel, and then I fill the tank again. On a couple of occasions, it started spitting and sputtering after getting gas at a particular station. *Oh, crud*, I thought. *Something bad is happening to my car.* I was triggered to panic. Generally, when this happens, I don't see the big picture. When I'm afraid, survival habits kick in, and I focus on one small piece of information in order to gain control and manage the situation. Twice my car died within a block or two of that station. I didn't know it at the time, but the real issue was not my engine malfunctioning but inferior gas that was polluted with condensation. I stopped feeding my car polluted fuel, and it ran great again. This is how my RAS works, too: clean VAKOG in, optimal function; polluted VAKOG in, subpar performance.

I am learning to feed my RAS clean VAKOG moment by moment. To build this skill, I started with short practice sessions of noting my mental activity. At first I did this by doing ten- to fifteen-minute guided meditations each morning, using the Headspace app. Then I started to build moments of noting into the day. Since my mind had been running on polluted VAKOG for much of my life, I had to be patient. The goal for me was awareness—to notice what was going on between my ears, stop the mind activity if it was polluted, and adjust myself. I now have a goal to quiet my mind and note mental activity for one to five minutes each hour. This helps me become detached from emotion, enabling me to make better VAKOG choices. I consciously choose high-quality pictures, movies, internal monologues, feelings, and sensations to feed my RAS.

When I catch myself being triggered and running polluted VAKOG, I mentally say something like, *Wow, this trigger is a great opportunity to heal another piece from the past! I am brave enough to quiet my mind and wait for inspiration. I am calm enough to listen without reacting to my feelings or thoughts. I have the courage to change my mind and experience new pictures in my head. I am resourceful. I easily change my internal monologue. Feelings aren't facts, they are just emotional information. This situation is temporary. The moment I'm living right now was created by past thought, and the past is over. I am creating a new life right this minute, and it is outrageous! I am grateful! I am changing my mind, and it feels awesome.*

I reorient myself, practice these kinds of soundbites, and quickly run my list of clean VAKOG images. But consistently feeding our RAS clean VAKOG can be a little tricky because no one teaches us about VAKOG; no one is talking about it. It's also because the gap from where we are now and where we want to be creates tension, and that tension is uncomfortable. It can combine with other feelings like doubt and uncertainty, creating a snowball of polluted VAKOG that knocks us off balance.

When I am unaware and react to those pictures and feelings as if they are true, clarity is compromised and the internal monologue (auditory pollution) ramps up, adding to the VAKOG mix. Before I know it, I'm a mess. A single unchecked internal thought, such as *Who gave you permission to think up a better way of using your mind to produce abundance?* can derail clarity and my intention to run clean VAKOG through my mind. If I accept the pollution without question, I can spiral off track, become distracted, lose my focus, and feed my RAS polluted VAKOG.

It all happens super-fast, which is another reason why it is tricky to run clean VAKOG. In order for my RAS to perform the way I want, I have to *slow things down*, note what is going on, and make a choice. I literally have to stop what I am doing and review what is happening in my mind. What pictures am I seeing? What am I telling myself? What feelings are present, and where do I feel them? Then I ask myself, *Do you want to keep it or let it go?* When I ask this question, I already know the answer: I want to let it go and feel happy again. So the next course of action is to address the trigger with tapping and let it go. For me, tapping works. If I am overstimulated with polluted VAKOG, I get help.

Some of the polluted VAKOG we have stems from the play-pretend game that kids from alcoholic and dysfunctional homes learn, me included. In such an environment, I was trained to mentally convert intense negative information into something different, something that made sense to me. Then I could carry on with a semblance of normalcy. Basically, I was taught to pretend that whatever was happening was not *really* happening. Converting reality into a lie in order to survive is quite a skill. I have no judgment about it, just an awareness of the amazing skill it takes to live and grow in an alcoholic home. Since I am no longer a child living in that environment, I can employ awareness and the tool of tapping to disarm old, unproductive responses.

I understand now why running clean VAKOG is tricky. I used to become flooded and overwhelmed when I was triggered by a generalized childhood memory of confusion and learned helplessness. Now I tap out those BFMs and transform old, unprofitable memories and money habits into new ones.

Structural Tension

When I set a goal, there is a gap between where I am now and where I want to be. That gap is a place of "structural tension." All tension seeks resolution, but I had to learn to let that tension be so that my unconscious mind could resolve it. Robert Fritz, author of the book *Creating*, taught me this years ago, and it is simmering to the surface now. He writes:

> A basic principle found throughout nature is this: Tension seeks resolution. From the spiderweb to the human body, from the formation of the galaxies to the shifts of continents, from the swing of pendulums to the movement of wind-up toys, tension-resolution systems are in play.
>
> I call the relationship between the vision and current reality structural tension. During the creative process, you have an eye on where you want to go, and you also have an eye on where you currently are.
>
> There will always be structural tension in the beginning of the creative process, for there will always be a discrepancy between what you want and what you have. Why? Because creators bring into being creations that do not yet exist. Structural tension is a fundamental principle in the creative process. In fact, part of your job as a creator is to form this tension.[8]

We can learn to embrace the structural tension of where we are now and where we want to be instead of trying to figure out how to make things happen. That doesn't work. The RAS is a key. Feed it good stuff, and it brings us good stuff.

FACING STRUCTURAL TENSION

In the beginning, I was frustrated by the gap between where I was and where I wanted to be. I consistently defaulted to thoughts like *How will I close this gap?* In actuality, it is the unconscious mind that resolves structural tension, not conscious left-brained activities. Structural tension is a normal part of the creative process, and I found Fritz's definition and explanation reassuring. When I am in the middle of this change process, it is important for me to note the gap instead of denying, ignoring, or running from it.

The feelings that come up when facing the gap are opportunities for healing. Practicing mindfulness enables us to pause, note the gap between where we are now and where we want to be, and acknowledge the feelings that arise. For example, as I pursue my BHAG, I have to keep my eye on where I am now and where I want to be simultaneously. I am often *in* the gap, and *this is challenging*.

At one point early on in the transformation process, my checking account was lower than I desired because I was waiting for deposits to come in. I didn't want to hit my savings, and I didn't like the current visual image of my checking account on the computer screen. I particularly disliked the data sets that arose. Some of these feelings were fear, uncertainty, and doubt, or FUD,* that manifested as tension in my gut, and there was

---

* Gene Amdahl coined the term FUD in 1975. It is an acronym for fear, uncertainty, and doubt.

an internal monologue that went something like, *Oh no, it's not working. I thought I changed this money pattern.* I spiraled for a moment with more audio: *This isn't working; why try so hard? I should probably just give up; it'll never change.*

The monologue in my head was based on negative beliefs about myself. Brené Brown calls this storytelling response a "shitty first draft" (SFD). I identified that the monologue was taking place in my head, that it was me talking to me. Identifying it as such is a good sign in the skill-development process. I have come to understand that this is my self-talk and that I have to do something about it. The picture that came to mind was my computer screen and an image of my bank statement. Each system—visual, auditory, and kinesthetic—triggered the others. Suddenly I was in an unproductive response, my personal SFD of the moment. Worse than that was my awareness that I was feeding my RAS polluted VAKOG. By noting my response, I was able to make a mature assessment of the situation and change my self-talk. *This is temporary. This is structural tension. You are in the gap and creating something new, Mary. No need to react. Tap on those old reactions and heal them up. You're right on schedule.*

I see now that feeding polluted VAKOG to my RAS was an engrained habit and that I was good at it. I had difficulty rearranging early BFMs that I had adopted about myself and money—they were linked, and I didn't know how to untangle them. I tried for years, and nothing worked. There seemed to be an invisible barrier between me and the changes I wanted to make, but it was my RAS doing its job to protect me.

Worksheet: RAS

Do you feed your reticular activating system, your RAS, polluted or clean VAKOG?

_____

_____

_____

How do you know you produce this kind of VAKOG?

_____

_____

_____

How can you change unproductive mind habits?

_____

_____

_____

How do you practice mindfulness?

_____

_____

_____

How long does it take for you to notice the quality—polluted or clean VAKOG—of your internal monologue?

_____

_____

How do you respond to structural tension?

_____

_____

_____

Why is it tricky for you to run clean VAKOG?

_____

_____

_____

CHAPTER 7

Competence

❀ ❀ ❀

Competence is having a required skill, knowledge, qualification, or capacity.

In this chapter we will discuss competence, step 6 in crushing your obstacles. When I coached and trained call center reps at a printing company years ago, I learned to identify performance strengths and challenges of individuals based on a "competency map." We used this tool to amplify strengths and fill gaps in the shortest time possible. I recalled this information at the beginning of my process to crush obstacles and transform my mind and money with tapping. As a result, I created a basic competency map for myself so I would know where I was in skill acquisition. Back then, we called the levels sub-basic, basic, proficient, and advanced. Here I use the terms "unconsciously incompetent," "consciously incompetent," "consciously competent," and "unconsciously competent."

Levels of Learning

In this section, we will look at moving from incompetent to competent in transforming our mind and money habits. First, let's see what each of the terms means.*

UNCONSCIOUSLY INCOMPETENT

When I am unconsciously incompetent, I don't know what I don't know. I am easily triggered, run polluted VAKOG, flood often, and don't know how to change financial outcomes. I routinely feed my RAS inferior VAKOG. I am unable to envision a future different from the one I am currently living. I am hypnotized by current events. I vent negatively and often to anyone who will listen. Positive financial results are seldom, random, or sporadic. There is generally more month than paycheck. I feel bad about myself and my performance. I tell myself that I work hard for my money. I have not created a vision board. My mind runs on default settings and swirls or spirals with polluted VAKOG. I have a hard time figuring out what to do next to change my mind and finances. Sometimes I am in "somebody fix me!" mode. "Tap? What's that?" You do it for me. I am constantly confused and disgusted. My resolve and owning of outcomes wavers. I am unaware of my body's stress response system and cortisol levels and how they impact my well-being. I occasionally meditate. I often review my bank accounts, bills, and debt, knowing there is not enough. I hold beliefs such as *It's never going to change. There will never be enough money. There's no time to do self-care. I have to make more money!*

---

* To learn more about these psychology terms, see the entry "Four stages of competence" at *Wikipedia*: https://en.wikipedia.org/wiki/Four_stages_of_competence.

Consciously Incompetent

When I am consciously incompetent, I know I need to feed my RAS by seeing and being in my preferred present, but I am not very good at it. Running clean VAKOG is work. Running polluted VAKOG is a habit. I am diligent. Flooding is less frequent. My confidence is building. I consciously feed my RAS in specific training moments, but I still default to polluted VAKOG 50 percent of the time. I created a vision board, but it's only sparsely filled in. I visualize the future from time to time. My resolve is at 100 percent, but I still waver on taking ownership of the outcomes. More money is appearing in my bank account, which sometimes surprises and shocks me. This is working, but I'm still not sure how. Yay! I feel hopeful. I tap sporadically to clear the polluted VAKOG when I am triggered. I am responsible. I am aware of my stress response system and cortisol levels, but I am not exactly sure how to reduce them. I meditate one or two times per week. I still mentally calculate how much is in my accounts, and I wonder if I have "enough" after paying bills or making purchases. I schedule occasional self-care activities.

Consciously Competent

When I am consciously competent, I feed my RAS by seeing myself as prosperous and being prosperous in my thoughts 75 percent of the time. This is getting easier, although it still takes mental focus. I watch my thoughts and reactions to people, places, and things, and release immediately with tapping. I tap on myself daily, and I get help when I am flooded. My income is steadily growing. I have 100 percent more money than before. I review my vision board daily, and I see, hear, feel, taste, and smell each reference as though it is right here, right now.

I visualize the future at the same time as I walk through the real-time day. I note and accept structural tension as a normal part of the transformation process. I meditate daily and run clean VAKOG when I get triggered. I am enthusiastic and excited. Flooding seldom happens. I consciously feed my RAS quality inputs numerous times a day. I am starting to "see" the RAS filtering aspects of prosperity into my awareness. I practice gratitude daily and give more of myself to others in time, money, and attention. I routinely schedule weekly self-care activities.

Unconsciously Competent

When I am unconsciously competent, I feed my RAS clean VAKOG and quality inputs 90 percent of the time, and doing so is my mental default. I quickly see my preferred present as though I am in it right now. I am enough, I have plenty, and I experience abundance when I think of my finances in real time. I have more money in the bank each month. I am debt-free or on my way there. I give freely and often. I tithe regularly. I run clean VAKOG and routinely feed my RAS a healthy diet of success, support, purpose, and abundance. I discuss my visioning for the future with a coach, mentor, or trusted others. I schedule daily meditations and experience spontaneous meditation moments during the day. My RAS is programmed now, and it brings to my attention inspiring VAKOG that propels me to prosperity outcomes with ease. I take at least one day off a week and schedule self-care activities two or three times per week. I take vacations one or more times per year. My stress response system and cortisol levels are easily identified and optimized. I have plenty of time and money to help others in need. I am financially fit, grateful, and happy.

Use these levels of learning to see the polluted VAKOG you run so you can tap daily to release the old beliefs you have about money and give yourself permission to envision a life of plenty. I found specific early childhood memories that supported old, polluted beliefs, then I tapped until the SUDS was 0 and the memory had zero negative emotions remaining. The greater issue for me was giving myself permission to envision a different future and permission to create an identity different from the girl who lived through a warzone.

I see now that feeding polluted VAKOG to my reticular activating system was an engrained habit and that I was good at it. At first, I had difficulty rearranging early beliefs, feelings, and memories I had adopted about myself (number one) and money (number two). I had tried for years, and nothing worked. It seemed like there was an invisible barrier between me and the changes I wanted. By grace, my answer was provided when I learned about VAKOG, RAS, and tapping. The past really is over.

I learned to let go of my old money mindset and feelings of low self-worth by tapping polluted VAKOG down to zero. Then I literally tapped in my preferred vision for the future, which I included on my vision board. The activity of "see it and be it" became fun homework, but I had to tap out feelings of guilt for wanting a new experience with myself and money and tap out any resistance to affluence. As I fed my RAS incredible images of hope and prosperity, life started changing around me.

Finally, I started to feel competent. The practice of consistently noting my thoughts, data sets, recurring BFMs, and tapping in the moment was building my skill and changing my mind. My RAS started responding to the clean VAKOG

I had been feeding it, bringing to my awareness and my life the items on my vision board. I started checking them off one by one, excited that I was getting better at transforming thoughts of myself and money. Prosperity results started showing up, first in little things like noticing all the good people and love I have in my life, and then bigger things, like more money coming in from new clients, book sales, speaking engagements, and workshops. My tank was filling up with the good stuff of life, and the more I noticed it, the more it appeared. I routinely expressed gratitude and found delight in the smiles and interactions of those around me. I was more generous, and I felt contentment and satisfaction for days, then weeks, at a time. I was happy with my progress.

Probably the biggest benefit from crushing my obstacles was crushing the negative internal monologue I used to produce. I used to say mean things to myself, and I didn't even know it. I marvel at how the brain works and how important I am in the equation of VAKOG and the outcomes I experience in my life. The efficiency of my RAS to filter and seemingly produce the good experiences I had always dreamed of is remarkable. Prosperity, inner certainty, and feeling rich in all the things that matter from the inside out started to become habits. The crushing process was transforming me and everything on the path in front of me. There were still a few BFMs to clear, but with focus and a growing competence, I knew I could do it.

Worksheet: Competence

In what areas of your life have you acquired advanced skills in being unconsciously competent?

_____
_____
_____

In what areas of your life are you unskilled, or unconsciously incompetent?

_____
_____
_____

How do the levels of learning relate to your self-esteem and money mindset?

_____
_____
_____

What competence level are you at with your mind habits?

_____
_____
_____

What competence level are you at with your money habits?

_____
_____

How can you increase your competence in areas where you are unskilled?

_____

_____

_____

How will this information help you transform your mind and money habits?

_____

_____

_____

CHAPTER 8
Focus

● ● ●

To focus is to direct one's attention or efforts.

In order to crush your obstacles, you must master step 7, staying focused on the goal to make the desired changes, no matter what. I realized that there were a couple of steps missing between seeing my dreams come true and having them be true. As I was working to "see it and be it" moment by moment, I hit a block. Instead of avoiding the obstacle, I chose to focus and got to work. I could see my audacious financial goal and visually imagine my life with high self-esteem, prosperity, and connection with the people, places, and things on my vision board, but I didn't believe that I could *be* the change. On top of that, even if I were to believe the clean VAKOG I was running through my mind, I still had another data set that said, *I can't receive*. What a silly program; of course I could—and did—receive. I simply wanted to receive more of the good stuff.

Since the past is over and my old concepts of believe and receive are polluted data sets, it is my job to change them immediately. I tapped on "I can't believe my dreams and goals are coming true," and my resistance rated a 10. I tapped that resistance down to a 1-2 and then got stuck; the belief wouldn't change to zero. Being on a compressed timeline, I reached out to practitioner friends Rita Duncan and Christin McLeod. One did a belief-change exercise from NLP, and the other did a visioning exercise that collapsed the bulk of my polluted data set about believing. I now had new pictures, movies, sounds, feelings, and sensations to replace the former data set.

I learned to not-believe when I was around three years old. I found this out when I closed my eyes and searched around for an early memory. I found a flash of a toddler picture that came to mind, but mostly it was a knowing. It felt 100 percent true that I "should not and could not believe." I seemed to have an invisible bubble around me that wouldn't let the good stuff in, wouldn't let me believe. I adopted it as fact back then, and one day this toddler image popped to the surface for release, which was good news. I now choose to believe all things are possible, and that includes letting go of disbelief.

I was challenged by the daily vision board exercise because I didn't have internal permission to dream really big. That has now changed. When I learned about the levels of learning (from the last chapter), I saw that the core competency of "see it and be it" involves the routine practice of seeing my dreams come true, as though they are happening in real time. On the night I finished my vision board, I made a commitment to review it three times per day for at least five minutes at a time. As I do this exercise frequently, what I notice is that I look around in hopeful expectancy for the good things to come. I don't spend time worrying about how it will happen. I leave that to the big guy upstairs and my RAS; its machine-like focus is flawless. I love this work!

Systematically running clean VAKOG through my brain is a new skill. It takes focus, so it can be a challenge. At the end of the day, I know I have worked hard because my body and mind are spent, but the fruits of my labors are showing up, and my mind is changing. My RAS is responding to clean VAKOG by bringing the items on my vision board to my attention: "Oh, look, there's my new truck," or "Oh, look over there, it's one of your book principles." I might get a call from a friend who wants to buy a copy of *Crush Your Obstacles* right now, and inspirations come out of the blue to pitch to television producers at the National Publicity Summit. While I am sitting next to a pickle maker in my business class, a thought arises that I want tapping to be like pickles: everyone knows what a pickle is. Not everyone knows what tapping is yet, but they will!

There is an element of anxiety in me these days, and I think it is excitement—these two feelings are so close to each other in emotional value that I'm going with excitement. Numerous times each day I ask, *What is the next right action for me to take? Where is my focus?* I am glad I need to focus only on this twenty-four-hour period. Having the past in its place, behind that amazing door I constructed, is a comfort. I now have more emotional ability to respond and to run clean VAKOG no matter what I am walking through in my outer world.

My next right action is to focus on my BHAG, my big, hairy, audacious goal. The practice of staying focused on this is a skill. I have to focus, let go, focus, let go. I have been used to *thinking* to get things done, and now I just feed my RAS clean VAKOG and let go to get things done. The structural tension is resolved by the unconscious mind. It is a very different method of operation: cognitive versus unconscious. It feels weird and counterintuitive to set a goal, feed my RAS clean VAKOG, vision my desired outcome, sincerely feel the goal completely done in record time, and then *let go*. Trusting goal completion to a side of me I haven't known very well is an act of faith.

I finalized my vision board with pictures of the people I love—my inspirations. I "live into" a millionaire richness as I view the love in my life right in this moment, regardless of revenue. This is one of my biggest learnings, that I am wealthy beyond compare when I focus on the amazing life I have right here and now: health, family, work, a relationship with my God, a home, plenty of money in the bank, and the ability to see beauty around me in the clouds, mountains, and sky. This is true wealth, and when I can feel it inside me daily, it can't help but show up on the outside.

I see my dreams, goals, and hope for the immediate future through my vision board. I physically see the pictures; good. It's a fact that I see the images. Now for the *be it* part: there can be a little turbulence here. I imagine removing an ugly old coat of beliefs, feelings, and memories and then stepping into a different one, a coat of possibility. This leads to a probability amplitude. *Where did that come from?* I ask myself. It came from listening to Deepak Chopra's book *Creating Affluence: Wealth Consciousness in the Field of All Possibilities* many years ago. I had the book and tape and listened to it as I drove across the moments and miles of my life, kids in tow, so it is wired into their brains, too. Bits of info pop up from time to time as soundbites, such as, *Where will all the money come from? From wherever it is at the moment.* That thought reminds me that for years I have been loading the mental pipeline with rich fuel to change myself and my financial outcomes.

Here is what I do to *be it*, to be bold, courageous, and prosperous in my mind: I imagine stepping into my vision board, and I make up a movie. I allow the two-dimensional pictures to rise up in front of me and become 3D. I set the timer for five minutes and walk the streets of my preferred present with all my senses alive, enjoying five minutes of pure, unadulterated bliss. Behind me on the vision board is an infinity pool. In slow motion I lie back into gold, pink, and teal. I breathe in, and it is done. Several times a day I step into my vision board and am immersed in the beauty, relief, and prosperity, rich in all the ways that matter. Focus, with clean VAKOG, is becoming a delightful respite.

The vision board experience, for me, is like stepping through the portal on *Stargate Atlantis*. On one side is my real-time world, and as I step through the portal into the 3D world of my vision board, I enter a new planet: my preferred present. It is filled with the good stuff I previously imagined. As a sci-fi geek, I love using the portal to walk into my preferred present. This focused neurological activity wires new networks in my brain, and at the same time, it makes me feel happy, light, spontaneous, and ready. As I walk through the portal, I see, hear, feel, and know that my goal is accomplished and that the journey was a blast. It was all that I hoped for and more.

In this version of my present, I rocked my SMART money goal and blew by it, creating more than I had expected. I notice that it wasn't the money that I wanted, it was the freedom to give of my time and money to causes and concerns that need financial support. Achieving my BHAG represents a huge shift in my self-value, and with the economic increase, I have plenty of time to share with kids and grandkids and to be helpful to them and others. In this place, my mind is quiet, and I am content. Walking this vision board is an exceptional adventure.

I step back through the portal into real time and plunk myself into bed. It is a great day to live with focus. *It'll get easier*, I coach myself with kindness and encouragement. As I advance in proficiency, the skill of changing my mind in the moment to clean VAKOG will become automatic. For now, it is stay focused, practice, see and be my vision board, and tap when I'm stuck.

Worksheet: Focus

Make a vision board using magazines, glue, and some kind of hard surface to glue your images to. Set a date for when you will complete it.

_____

_____

_____

How do you feel about the pictures on your vision board?

_____

_____

_____

Can you imagine the pictures on your vision board coming to life in 3D?

_____

_____

_____

How strong is your ability to "see it and be it" with regard to your vision board?

$0 =$ not strong and $10 =$ very strong

Make a date with yourself to review your vision board.

When you are triggered to negativity, how do you get out of it?

_____

_____

_____

How long does it take to shift to clean VAKOG?

_____

_____

_____

What does the word "focus" mean to you with respect to changing your mind and money habits?

_____

_____

_____

CHAPTER 9

Persevere

● ● ●

To persevere is to persist in anything undertaken; to maintain a purpose in spite of difficulty, obstacles, or discouragement; or to continue steadfastly.

Each step toward crushing your obstacles is vital in your success, and step 8, perseverance, is crucial. Some days the process of owning our responses to life and changing to clean VAKOG on the spot can feel like wrestling. When an old response rears up, we have an immediate choice to make: do we want to be right or be happy? Do we want to keep it or let it go? We can choose to quickly neutralize negative responses in our minds before we speak or act. To continue with the wrestling metaphor, there might be moments in the match where we feel pinned by external triggers and default responses, but by consciously choosing a different way to think and act in the moment, things can turn around quickly, and we can on top again. Then the match is over.

Figure 2. Visual reminder

I put visual reminders like the one in figure 2 everywhere: on my desk, in my car, next to my bed, in the bathroom. They create an immediate mental shift because they represent the expanse of the unconscious mind that is created by peace of mind and my creator. Changing my thoughts is still work at this level, but I am making progress. I know this because when an event happens with another person in my outer world, I now have the skill to pause, catch my reaction, and adjust my attitude. I am aware that my old response is coming from something in the past. I don't even have to know where it is coming from if I stay focused on my desired outcome: a quiet, satisfied mind. Then I quickly go through my checklist and ask myself, *Do I have resolve?* Yes. *Am I 100 percent responsible for my life and responses?* Yes. *Am I ready to change?* Yes! *Am I willing to tap on polluted VAKOG and identify my BFMs?* Yes.

Healing Reactions

As I release old BFMs, physical and emotional responses come up. Robert Smith, the creator of FasterEFT, says that these responses are the body's reaction to perception, and this seems true for me. During the days and weeks that I was creating my vision board, I got pink eye. My lower back almost went out, I got a stomach bug, and I had various other bodily reactions to the metaphorical work I was doing. My response? I owned the reactions and tended to them as best I could. I didn't speak negatively about the situations or events to anyone because they were just healing reactions.

When I am up and able, I tap, often using Louise Hay's book *Heal Your Body A–Z* to identify a metaphorical meaning for the distress I was experiencing. Hay describes the eyes as representing "the capacity to see clearly—past, present, and future." This description is spot on with respect to embracing the vision board process. The lower back represents "fear of money and lack of financial support." Again, my body was right on target with releasing beliefs about money and finances. Regarding stomach problems, she writes, "Dread. Fear of the new. Inability to assimilate the new"[9]—another bullseye.

Preverbal Data Sets

I used to get stuck in overwhelm or flooded feeling states until I learned about preverbal data sets.* I coined this term as an explanation for what was happening to me when I was triggered by something from childhood.

Preverbal data sets are beliefs, feelings, and memories from early childhood. They are unique because the language associated with them isn't very well developed, but the feelings are. When I hit a confusing trigger and I can't explain it—I just "know" it—it is a sign that I am accessing a preverbal data set consisting of self-esteem and money beliefs that were solidified in early childhood. It would be a broad brush stroke to say that all of our beliefs were set at that time, but I would venture to say that 90 percent of our beliefs were created by the time we were seven years old.

---

*"Preverbal data set" is a term I coined to describe "packets" of information formed during early childhood that seldom have words to describe the belief, feeling, or memory at hand.

As a healing reminder of my old, preverbal data sets, I keep a picture of myself at age five on my rear-view mirror to remind me to integrate that little girl into my current life and let her know that the tough stuff from the past is over. I also tap daily on BFMs from early childhood, and as a result, I no longer feel like a little kid in a room full of adults, which is new for me. To illustrate, I was at a Christmas program for my granddaughter the other day. As I sat waiting for the show to start, I looked around the room, noticed all the other folks, and realized that I felt calm and content—right-sized. I felt normal, like the adult I am, instead of a scared, nervous, and socially anxious woman. In the past, I felt small in certain settings. With tapping and mindfulness, I am starting to feel comfortable in my own skin.

Mindspace

Mindspace is the place inside the head where all thought action takes place. At the beginning of this process to change my mind, I had to know what was going on in there. Meditation was the answer for me, but I am not talking about the kind of meditation where you sit on a little round pillow on the floor and stare at a wall; that must be for more advanced meditators. I'm talking about the kind of meditation where you simply stop producing thoughts and focus on breathing. At first I had difficulty quieting my thoughts without assistance, so I found a couple of apps with a wide variety of guided meditations; I still listen to them daily (see Resources).

As a result, meditation has changed the way I interact with myself and the world. I am adopting focus by learning to let go of all the thoughts in my head and just watch them go by. It is strange to me that quieting the mind produces focus and perseverance. Before I created a meditation practice, I was unconsciously incompetent at quieting my mind. Now that I am gaining skill with it and am more proficient, I am probably at conscious incompetence, with a dash of acceptance and objectivity.

Noting

"Noting"* is an activity in which we detach, watch our thoughts, and "note" when we are thinking, feeling, idling between thoughts and activity, remembering, reacting, or rehearsing. By saying aloud, "I'm thinking," "This is a feeling," "I'm thinking about a memory now," "I'm idle now," and so on, we build awareness of what has always been an unconscious activity. Anchoring prosperity and transforming our minds in the shortest amount of time requires a persevering focus and clarity about what we are thinking and feeling. Noting builds our awareness and slows the cognition process, interrupting default thinking to enable new choices. We can ask ourselves, *Do I want to keep thinking this thought, feeling, memory, or reaction? Is it helping me feel better right now?* If our thoughts are on auto-pilot and we don't know what is going on in our heads, our choices are reduced and focus is unspecified. When this happens, I often don't even realize the need for focus because I am engaged with the current thought activity, usually a BFM or a reaction.

Meditation and noting make it possible to clarify what is happening in our minds and help us persist toward our goals. I used to avoid spending time with myself in this kind of quiet

---

Headspace co-founder Andy Puddicombe frequently reminds subscribers about the activity of "noting" during guided meditations.

activity because I was afraid to get to know myself, but now I feel more control as I learn to detach, note my thoughts, and let go of thinking for specific periods of time each day. It makes all the difference.

Worksheet: Persevere

How do you persevere through hard challenges to complete a goal?

_____
_____
_____

How long does it take for you to shift out of polluted VAKOG: minutes, hours, days, weeks? _____

What mind or money habit do you want to change? What challenges might arise while you are changing it?

_____
_____
_____

Go through the checklist:

Do you have resolve? _____

Are you 100 percent responsible for your life and responses?

_____
_____

Are you ready to change? _____

Will you tap on polluted VAKOG and the BFMs that impact your mind and money experiences? _____

Why or why not?

_____

_____

_____

What do you think about preverbal data sets?

_____

_____

How often are you negatively triggered by something from early childhood?

_____

_____

_____

What is your mindspace like today? How would you like your mindspace to be?

_____

_____

_____

CHAPTER 10
Believe

To believe is to have confidence in the truth, the existence, or the reliability of something without absolute proof that one is right in doing so.

Believing in ourselves, believing that we can create, change, be, and receive what we want, is the essence of step 9. The state of prosperity, to me, is believing in "more than enough." Prosperity means plenty of time, money, food, energy, health, freedom, and space to live with purpose and dignity. In this state, we give freely of what we have to offer because we have more than enough. We laugh often and feel freedom from tension in our bodies and minds, and any pressure we feel goes away, erased by gratitude.

To me, the main features of prosperity are a quiet mind and an inward knowing that all is well; absolutely everything springs from this place of peace (which is my understanding of God). I simply *believe* that there is enough, and I am deeply satisfied. It sounds too easy to be true, but it's not. It used to be hard to believe in a future that I had not yet experienced, and stating a future goal and then letting go of my attachment to that goal took conscious effort. Doing this runs counter to the way we are taught in school and in life. Believing in and having confidence in things that are unseen are based on acting *as if* the goal is already achieved. Once I got the hang of believing, good things quickly started coming my way. But I had to govern my thoughts carefully during the beginning stages of believing, because I was erratic, like a kid learning to ride a bicycle. I used to be such a doubter, and the thought activity of self-doubting was unconscious and chronic.

Believing is not an intellectual activity for me; it is completely feeling-based, which was why it was work. I had to *feel* belief in my body and then act *as if* the goal were done. Here are some of the things I did (and continue to do) to stay positive and believe that all things are possible:

- I immersed myself in positive thoughts through prayer, scripture, meditation, pictures, my vision board, and connecting with others of like mind. If I didn't have anyone nearby, I checked out options at the library or at gatherings like the Women's Prosperity Network and Positive Thinking meetups.
- I disconnected from negative people, conversations, and activities.
- I joined a mastermind group of prosperity-minded people to foster growth.

- I found an accountability partner with whom I could practice "conscious future pacing."* We talked to each other "as if" our goals were achieved. Having another person listen and *believe* in me is a powerful practice.
- I posted visual reminders about belief, possibilities, encouragement, and hope everywhere.
- I tapped on the earliest beliefs, feelings, and memories I could find that involved doubt, loss of hope, and giving up.
- I made a list of five positive memories from when I believed in something and it came true. I focused on the feelings, pictures, and positive elements of those memories to re-experience belief (and delight). I practiced this numerous times a day to feed my RAS and to imagine new neural pathways for "belief" and "believing."
- I practiced seeing, hearing, feeling, touching, smelling, and tasting the elements on my vision board as though they are already done and in my life. I still do this, and I tap during the exercise, imagining that I have the power to neurologically "set" my RAS to a positive filtering and sorting mode. For example, I frequently imagine walking through my new office, admiring the work stations, the people, the advanced technology, and the phone systems. I imagine tasting an excellent cup of coffee as I sit on the patio of my beachfront home, staring out at the waves, smelling the salty air as a warm breeze caresses my face. I imagine smiling

---

* "Conscious future pacing" is a term I coined to identify productive thought activity made of clean VAKOG that we project into the future.

as I look at my Fitbit and feeling grateful for my health and fitness.
- I practiced running clean VAKOG with image cycling.

The more I practice the rich detail of each desire or want, the stronger I feel it and the better I become at believing all things are possible.

One outstanding example of believing (before I was conscious of VAKOG) was when I was hired to sell printing around Montana. I was driving a vintage Oldsmobile Delta 88, a canary-yellow boat with no radio. Shortly after I started at the print shop, I was talking with a friend about vehicles. I said, "I want a Dodge Ram." He laughed and said, "Yeah, don't we all." I shrugged my shoulders and said, "Well, that's what I'd like," and let it go.

A few weeks later, I saw a Dodge Ram in a neighbor's driveway with a For Sale sign on it. *I wonder if it's supposed to be mine*, I thought. I called the number and spoke to the owner. It turned out that I used to take care of her mom. We chatted about her mom, the truck, and taking it for a test drive. I told her I had started a new job and needed a four-wheel-drive vehicle to travel the state.

We got along famously, and after a test drive, she said, "I'm going out of town. Why don't you park it in your driveway for the weekend? You can check on a loan, and we'll talk Monday." It was surreal to have that truck in my driveway. I had driven clunkers my whole life, and shifting into the belief that I was worthy and could own a late-model truck was unbelievable. The kids marveled that it even had a radio and a CD player!

I learned that I would need six months of pay stubs to get a loan. I called the woman and told her, and she said, "That's okay. What if you make the payments for the next six months and *then* get a loan—would that work? It seems like it's supposed to be yours, and we need to sell it."

Despite all odds, the truck was mine. Six months later, I got the loan, and everything went off without a hitch. Somewhere inside, I believed that I could have a Dodge Ram. I didn't spend any energy "making it happen"; I simply expressed the desire, then let it go and went on with my life.

That big, tangible Dodge Ram experience taught me the concept of *believe*. But how did it happen? First, I attribute it to grace. Next, I said a prayer, stated the goal to myself and another person, set the GPS of my intention on a Dodge Ram, and then *let it go*. My RAS was on the lookout. I had provided clean VAKOG and hadn't even known that was what I was doing.

The previous year, I had listened to Deepak Chopra's book *Creating Affluence, The A-to-Z Steps to a Richer Life*. We listened to it *a lot*. The kids pretended they were Deepak Chopra speaking of quarks and bosons, and they recited in their best Chopra voice many of the soundbites they heard. Looking back, I realize that the principles outlined in this book were manifesting in my life, as they are now. However, I got into a relationship back then that I thought was a path to a richer life; I lost my focus and put things aside. But that is a story for another time.

My Dodge Ram experience sums up this chapter: *believe*. Ask for what you want, believe that it can be yours, and receive it. It sounds simple, but I spent a bunch of years trying to figure out the mechanics of believing and receiving. The obstacle for me was a belief itself: I believed that I needed to know *intellectually* how things would come to pass. This became a default activity that unconsciously ran in the background of my life. The need to know how kept me stuck.

I wasn't clear about this belief until I sat down to write this chapter. Once I homed in on the target belief, the need-to-know-how, I used tapping to change it to *I trust. I have all the info I need now. When I need more, it will be given to me at the perfect time, right on time.* Every time I say this to myself, I am flooded with relief. I imagine my new neural networks lighting up, my neck and shoulders relaxing, and my cortisol levels dropping; I am at ease.

Now that I don't need to figure out the "how" of prosperity, I'm ready to move on to receiving. I check my work: *Did I set the destination on my GPS?* Yes. *Am I clear on my BHAG?* Quiet contentment in my mind and $365,000 in a year—check. *Am I cleaning up polluted VAKOG as it arises, exchanging it for clean VAKOG?* Check. *Did I consciously ask for this desire to be blessed?* Yes. *Do I have internal permission to proceed?* Yes.

Summing things up, my preferred present is to receive quiet contentment in my mind, to feel good about myself and the woman I have become, and to have my money thermostat set to more-than-enough; $365,000 in a year represents more-than-enough. I notice my preferred present, and at the same time, I let go of it like I did with the Dodge Ram. I tap on anything that comes up during my day that feels negative. I discard pollution and run clean VAKOG with tapping. I feel calm inside, quiet in my mind, and rich in all the things that matter. As I look around my life, I know that I am loved, and I am happy and grateful. This is my internal experience of prosperity, and each day it brings abundance into my material world. This is very different from the mind habits I used to have.

Now that I know I can (and must) produce calm, relaxed mental content via pictures, movies, sounds, feelings, and sensations, I am committed. I have faith in the unseen process of creation that brings life to my dreams. No matter what comes, I am a better person for converting polluted VAKOG into clean and pouring it through this mind. Refreshed by new thoughts, I am delighted and happy and attentive to the moment right in front of me.

These are some of the benefits of "believe." An inward confidence and ability has emerged as a result of using this simple ten-step guide to transformation with tapping. I trust now; this is a big deal. The little girl in the garage band who was able to believe long ago but then lost that ability is back! I have choices about what is going on in my head and a responsibility to choose kind thoughts about myself and others. I have also found a forgiving kindness toward my past and the people in it. I know for certain that it is long since over, and *that*, for me, is profound liberty.

I believe that all things are possible. I don't have to know *how* it will all come about. Straining, willing things to happen, pushing neurons around—that ineffective practice is now done. Results are on their way.

Worksheet: Believe

What is your definition of prosperity?
_____
_____

How do you feel about practicing "as if" your goals and dreams have already happened?
_____
_____

What do you currently believe about being able to transform your mind and money habits?
_____
_____

Can you remember a time when you wanted something with certainty, let go of it, and then had it come to you?
_____
_____

What do you think about your need to know *how* something is going to happen? Does it help or hinder you?
_____
_____

What do you absolutely believe is true about yourself and money?
_____
_____

CHAPTER 11
Receive

* * *

To receive is to meet with or to experience.

You can move through each of the steps described in this book, but without step 10, the ability to receive, your progress will halt right here. I watched the movie *The Secret* when it first came out in 2007 and numerous times since. Each time I saw it, I would get excited. The idea that "ask, believe, and receive" could happen felt tangible and possible, even for me. But I felt guilty admitting that I had wants. The monologue in my head said, *Just be happy with what you have.* When I dug a little deeper, it was more than guilt that I felt; I hadn't done anything wrong by desiring or even believing in a better life for me and my family, but to receive a better life? That concept ran distinctly counter to a hardened identity rooted in shame. I read Mark 11:24—*Therefore I tell you, whatever you ask for in prayer, believe that you have received it, and it will be yours*—and tried to understand and integrate the inner workings of receiving.

I hit a wall and couldn't write. Panic and anxiety rose to the surface, and I worked to quickly find the source of polluted VAKOG. Within hours, I had followed the emotional trail and identified a stout data set of old BFMs. Receiving and shame would not coexist. I looked up the difference between guilt and shame to clarify my emotional experience and found a blog on the subject by Brené Brown:

- I believe that there is a profound difference between shame and guilt. I believe that guilt is adaptive and helpful—it's holding something we've done or failed to do up against our values and feeling psychological discomfort.
- I define shame as the intensely painful feeling or experience of believing that we are flawed and therefore unworthy of love and belonging—something we've experienced, done, or failed to do makes us unworthy of connection.
- I don't believe shame is helpful or productive. In fact, I think shame is much more likely to be the source of destructive, hurtful behavior than the solution or cure."[10]

The people interviewed in *The Secret* must not have had any shame, because they made a prosperous mindset seem easy. My childish hope was that by simply watching the video or memorizing Mark 11:24, I would absorb new skills that would transform me and my finances forever. But doing the same thing over and over (memorizing the verse or repeatedly watching the movie and hoping) was not enough to change polluted VAKOG about money or me. I had to address the shame core with tapping in order to receive different results in my life.

The unconscious data set I discovered inside had been destructive and hurtful to me and my finances for as long as I could remember. This shame core was the source of my not-enough habits of mind, self, and money. It was also the reason I stopped reading *The Success Principles* back in 2016. Now, in order to receive my BHAG of a quiet, trusting mind and a life rich with all the things that matter, the shame core had to go.

I cycled through resolve, own, VAKOG, and RAS. With competence, focus, and perseverance, I got a little bit of support and set aside time to let that old data set go with tapping. I followed the quick-start action steps and named the issue "shame core": an intense, old data set consisting of BFMs that I am flawed, inadequate, unworthy, and unlovable. It was a picture that had numerous strong feelings attached and had a SUDS rating of 10. I tapped, changing the SUDS lower each round, and alternated with a series of happy, peaceful memories. When I got to zero, I could no longer find the shame core.

I made up a picture of what I would prefer to experience, called it "Core Brilliance," added sound and feeling, and tapped it in. This new data set of clean VAKOG has now been added to the images I cycle through my mind numerous times each day, reinforcing neural networks and creating new mind and money habits. With the experience of Core Brilliance alive inside me, I believe I can now receive.

To meet with and experience high esteem and plenty (the good stuff in life), we have to root out and change polluted VAKOG and data sets of shame, doubt, disbelief, and blame, and then replace them with clean VAKOG. We have to crush them in order to receive. These data sets sometimes seem stuck inside and can become elemental parts of our identity unless we take action and change them. When we clean up

BFMs from the past, especially doubts about self, value, and abilities, we are more present and able to help others. If you have a shame core and believe *I'm flawed, I'm not enough, I don't have enough*, and so on, you can change it with tapping.

I have felt rich in many areas of my life, but internal and financial prosperity was an enigma until I said "Enough," found resolve, and got to work. I had expected to make more than glacial progress in living my dreams, but that expectation only set me up to resent myself. This was one of the first BFMs to go. Some of the new internal monologues I hear now are, *I did the best I could with the tools that I had in the moment*, *It is what it is*, and *My time is now*. I am even starting to believe them through repetition.

As I watered the geraniums this morning, I realized that it was taking longer than usual. I untwirled the hose and found numerous kinks in it. *I've got to spend the money and get a decent hose*, I said in my head. Then I got it. *Oh, the hose. It's hooked up to the water supply, and the hose has kinks in it that are keeping the plants from receiving the water they need. Got it.* I have been running polluted VAKOG through my mental hose and expecting my financial results to magically change. If there are kinks in the hose, nothing is going to make that water come out more quickly except unkinking the hose.

Where are the kinks in the hose around receiving? I review my work. *Do I have resolve?* Yes. *Do I own my results and accept that I learned to run polluted VAKOG unchecked?* Yes. *Am I committed to running clean VAKOG right this moment?* Yes. *Can I see and be the life on my vision board?* Yes, I see it, but no, I don't really feel it. A little wavering. Okay. Check my day yesterday. *Did I review my vision board three times?* Ah-hem, nope. I was busy writing! There it is: fear, uncertainty, and doubt—FUD. *Do I want to keep it or let it go?* Let it go. *How do I let go of fear on an emotional level?*

Right, I trust. I have all the info I need right now. The past is over. I have never been here in this moment before. I stop what I am doing and internally assess my state. Fear and uncertainty rate at a 10. I tap. I can address this pollution even while I am sitting at a coffee shop. Nobody is looking. I get it down to a 6 in two rounds of tapping by alternating between clean and polluted VAKOG. I choose clean pictures, movies, and sounds that quickly help me access the most comfort and relaxation. Today it is being at the ocean and seeing blue-green water clear to the horizon.

I check the rating for my FUD, and it is down to a 4-5. I know this because I am visual and I see a 4-5 in my head, white numbers on a black background. I mentally change the numbers to rainbow colors and tap as I say, "Whatever I have made this mean, I let it go." Deep breath. Check FUD again. It is a 1-2. This time I know because I have a nervous feeling in my gut and the screen of my mind is blank and black. I switch for a second to the ocean in my mind. I feel the water, hear the laughter of my grandkids splashing, and see us walking up the pier to our cabana. Yeah, that feels good. This is my preferred present. I breathe in. I feel confident and relaxed knowing that my neural network just fired clean VAKOG. My shoulders drop, I feel the chair supporting me, and I know that I am right here, right now, and all is well. I am receiving! Nice work.

I check the FUD rating again. *Can you find it?* No. My mind clicks back to the ocean image, clean VAKOG. I check back in on the feeling that had been in my body just moments before, and I can tell that the fear is changing neurologically. I breathe in the imagined smell of the ocean and see its teal color.

I imagine my internal computer keyboard on the screen of my mind and hit the *Save* button, saving my neurological work like a Word document. Yay for clean VAKOG! I run the ocean image one more time for good measure, and gosh, that feels good. I just changed my mind. *This* is how I receive. *This* is how I meet with prosperity and accept it into my mind and my day as I sit in a coffee shop on a busy Montana morning. I am actively transforming my habits of mind and money with tapping!

Okay, back to the kinks in my mental hose. I look over the hose like it is my timeline, and I see a recurring kink: a relationship pattern that has distracted me from obtaining long-term financial goals. It is commingled with a victim mindset and low self-esteem. I formed these habits early on. Two data points equal a trend line, and three is a pattern. Wherever the hose wound around the hose holder (I checked; that's its name), there was a kink. The less expensive hose did not want to make that turn, so it kinked. *How is this a metaphor for me?* I ask. Each time I make a turn in my life, even now, I feel FUD: a deep fear of the unknown and of being alone. By this I mean *alone* alone—kids grown up, no dog to keep me company or keep me safe, the I'm-on-my-own-now kind of alone that echoes inside and makes me want to run.

When fear, uncertainty, and doubt appeared in the past, it triggered an old response: Fire up a relationship! Then I'll be too busy to feel the fear! I didn't have the coping skills or tools to address a recurring trigger as just that, a trigger. Now I know that this old response indicates a polluted data set comprising BFMs from the past. This is all it is. Now when fear and doubt appear, I try to welcome them as a healing opportunity instead of running from them. When I courageously address BFMs, healing comes, and I am changed.

The problem with the relationship pattern/FUD trigger is that I abandon myself and the hope of becoming comfortable in my own skin because I focus on *them* instead of me. When I run from BFMs from the past, the act of running deepens the kink and cuts off the water supply. When I am dealing with old triggers, it helps me to remember that *the past is over*; those moments are simply not real any longer. I remember that I have a protective door in my mind that is sealing off the past from my present, and I have everything I need in this moment because it is a new moment. I have never been here before. When I run clean VAKOG, *bam!* I'm back in the present moment, back in receiving mode. Sometimes shifting from the old mind set to knowing that I am truly the only one responsible for this life shocks me. I must learn to receive with dignity and gratitude. It all starts in my mind.

I accept the kinks in my timeline as growth opportunities that are rich in learnings. The process of reframing past events and patterns into productive data sets helps me better manage my life. I feel hopeful, and I know I am not the only one who grapples with the gap between where we are now and where we want to be financially, emotionally, or physically. I am comforted to know I am not alone.

My perception of receiving has changed. I am excited to set the GPS on my goal, as though I am taking a trip. I like knowing that I will get there in a certain amount of time yet not knowing the terrain I will pass through until I am passing through it. The act of receiving used to make me feel uncomfortable, vaguely out of control and unnerved. I checked the definition of "unnerved": to cause to lose courage, strength, confidence, and self-control. Apparently, that unnerved feeling triggered the habitual response of running from myself and hiding in relationship. This *added* obstacles to my path instead of crushing them.

As I finish writing this, I notice a loosening of the inner controls that governed my thoughts and actions about giving, receiving, self-value, and money. Meditation teaches me that I receive a quiet mind when I note the thoughts going through my head and detach from mental pursuits for a time. This helps me make better choices. When I experience an unquiet mind, I am unresourceful, so I breathe, talk to God, and turn to tapping as soon as possible. With a quiet mind, I respond instead of react. This changes my outcomes.

Tapping teaches me that:

- I can change beliefs, feelings, and memories in the heat of the moment.
- I initiate my mental and emotional responses, for good or bad.
- It is my responsibility to change polluted VAKOG as soon as possible.
- I am free to make new choices that allow me to live my preferred present.
- Doing this cleanup work is the best, most honorable thing I can do for myself, my family, and the world.

I'm getting a new hose today. No more kinks. No more obstacles. I receive prosperity on the inside; it is only a thought away.

Worksheet: Receive

What beliefs, feelings, and memories are obstacles that need to be cleaned up in order to change your mind about yourself and money?

_____
_____
_____

Do you have any "shame core" data sets you want to release and let go?

_____
_____
_____

Where are the kinks in the hose around your ability to receive?

_____
_____
_____

What are your fears, uncertainties, and doubts about yourself?

_____
_____
_____

What are your fears, uncertainties, and doubts about money?

_____

_____

_____

What do you currently do about these FUD?

_____

_____

_____

How would you like to respond to FUD in the future?

_____

_____

_____

Epilogue

Crush Your Obstacles is an internal mandate that drove me to find a solution to transform thoughts about myself and my money habits. Tapping is the tool I used over and over to address beliefs, feelings, and memories from the past, and I still use it. Knowing that the past really is over and that I have control over how much it affects me builds my esteem and confidence.

The process of change is an inside job for which we are 100 percent responsible. The main elements I use to "embrace the suck" of polluted VAKOG and transform it to clean VAKOG with tapping are resolve and commitment to be a better person. Daily practice of quieting my mind and reviewing my vision board empower me to dream really big and believe that I am worth the effort.

My preferred present is a lovely dream that happens while I am awake. It is a constructed series of pictures, movies, feelings, sensations, and internal monologues that are helpful, positive, and uplifting. It builds my self-esteem and value, enabling me to achieve my BHAG. On a day-to-day level, my preferred present is simply a choice that stems from an answer to the question, *What would I prefer to experience right now, in this moment?* We seldom ask this question of ourselves, yet it can reveal what we want and need during a particular moment in time.

In my preferred present, obstacles are crushed. There is plenty of time, money, and love to go around, plenty to share. There always was, and I didn't know it. My financial thermostat is now set to more-than-enough and plenty. I *can* receive; I *am* receiving. I am finally comfortable in my own skin. I used to wonder when that would happen, and now, here it is. I "walk like a pilot,"[u] like I own the place where I live and move. With the door to my personal past closed, I am resourceful and able to meet life on life's terms. With clean VAKOG in, clean VAKOG out, who will I be as I live my preferred present and teach others to find theirs? Happy. Grateful. Ready to be of service.

APPENDIX

How to Find Resolve

To find resolve, first identify the earliest negative beliefs, feelings, and memories (BFMs) that are standing in your way. Think of the earliest experience you can remember. Earliest is best, as then things change faster. Those early BFMs are what anchored my current negative financial state (see table 1).

To find your resolve, follow these steps:

- Write out your BFMs.
- Determine your current (inner) overall experience of resolve to crush your obstacles to prosperity. (I will use "I can't find resolve" from table 1 as an example throughout these steps.)
- Note the SUDS to your resolve: 0 = no resolve 10 = I am absolutely determined
- Find your strongest emotional response from your list of BFMs. ("It's no use; it works for them but not for me.")
- SUDS this response.

- Tap it out. For the first round, really *feel* the feelings. ("I am one year old and can't walk. They can, I can't.") Name the feelings while tapping on the four points:
- I'm letting go of this belief. ("It's no use; it works for them but not for me.") I am letting go of all the frustration, hopelessness, helplessness, feeling of giving up, having no resolve, anger, desperation, disgust, worthlessness, sadness, fear, resentment, shame, the feeling that I can't do it. All of this and everything else that blocks my resolve to crush obstacles to financial prosperity—I am letting it all go now.
- Squeeze your wrist, take a deep breath, say boom, it's done, peace, shazam, or any word that marks completion for you.
- Go to a calm, confident, peaceful memory. Make it really good (no pollution). Take a deep breath, squeeze your wrist, and say "peace."
- SUDS it again. ("It's no use; it works for them but not for me.") Note the number. It should be lower than before.
- Tap it out.
- This belief is no use. ("I'm letting it go. I'm not one year old anymore, let it go, let it go, let it go.")
- Squeeze your wrist and say "peace."
- Bring forth a calm, confident, peaceful memory. See it, hear it, feel it, be there. Take a deep breath and say "peace."
- SUDS it again. ("It's no use; it works for them but not for me.") Note the number. It should be lower.

Repeat this process until you zero it out.

Table 1. Steps to finding resolve

Resolve		
Beliefs	Feelings	Memories
I can't find resolve.	Frustration, hopelessness, helplessness	I'm four years old, and I can't get my picture to turn out like theirs. It's no use. (I see this as a movie.)
Even if I have it, nothing will change.	Wanting to give up, anger, desperation	I'm in fifth grade. I got Danny's attention, but nothing changed. He still likes her better than me. (I see this as a picture.)
I'm a failure. I can't get the picture of their faces out of my head.	Disgust, worthlessness, shame, fear	I'm three years old. I knock a glass off the table, and Mom and Dad are super angry. (I hear the sound of glass breaking. I see their faces.)
I never get what I want. I don't deserve it. I can't have it even though I want it. I may as well give up.	Sadness, fear, resentment, disappointment	I'm in seventh grade. I want a new bike like Sarah. I am determined to get it. It doesn't come for Christmas. (I see Sarah's bike.)
It's no use; it works for them but not for me. I can't do it. Boys are better, faster, and smarter than me.	Helplessness, hopelessness, shame	I'm one year old. I keep falling down. My twin brother is walking. It works for him but not for me. (I see a movie of him walking and me falling down. I have a knowing that I can't do it.)

Glossary

BFMs: Beliefs, feelings, and memories.

Target BFM: One belief, feeling, or memory to target for change with tapping.

Data set: A bundle of beliefs, feelings, and memories that are neurologically wired together.

Flooding: Extreme overwhelm with disordered thoughts and an unmanageable abundance of feelings, beliefs, and memories.

Future pacing: A neurolinguistic programming term for mentally imagining a future event. I created the following distinctions to help clarify mental activity so I can make a choice:

Negative future pacing: Imagining a future event to be negative.

Positive future pacing: Imagining a future event to be positive.

Unconscious future pacing: Imagining future events without knowing you are doing so.

Idling: Passing time doing nothing; the space between conscious thought activity and unconscious thought activity.

Looping: Recycling a thought; repeating a word, phrase, or idea in the background of the mind, with or without awareness, for no apparent reason.

Noting: Observing thoughts and feelings with objectivity, detachment, and acceptance as they pass through the screen of the mind.

Pollution: Contamination, unproductive thoughts.

Preferred present: A term I coined to describe a lovely dream that happens while we are awake; a constructed series of pictures, movies, feelings, sensations, and sounds that feed the RAS until the desired outcome is achieved.

RAS (reticular activating system): A part of the brain that sorts and filters information into bite-sized bits so the important stuff gets through.

Reference: A memory; something that has already transpired.

Reframing: Changing the way we perceive a person, place, or thing.

Shame core: An intense, old data set consisting of BFMs that "I am flawed, inadequate, unworthy, and unlovable."

Structural tension: The relationship between our vision and current reality.

SUDS: Subjective Units of Distress Scale, a measurement tool to determine the intensity of a belief, feeling, or memory so it can be changed. 0 = not at all; 10 = strong

Tapping: A tool used to release stress and unproductive patterns of beliefs, feelings, and memories.

Thought habits: A pattern of mental activity that is regularly followed until it has almost become involuntary.

Trigger: An internal or external event that activates a negative belief, feeling, or memory that then produces an unproductive response.

Unresourceful: The inability to deal skillfully and promptly with events, beliefs, feelings, and memories.

VAKOG: An acronym for visual, auditory, kinesthetic, olfactory, and gustatory information.

- **Clean VAKOG:** Clear, uplifting, resourceful pictures, movies, sounds, feelings, sensations, smells, and tastes we remember or construct in order to create a positive state.
- **Polluted VAKOG:** Contaminated pictures, movies, sounds, feelings, sensations, smells, and tastes we remember or construct and that create a negative state.

Zero it out: To neutralize a belief, feeling, or memory to a SUDS zero intensity with tapping.

Resources

MARY CASSIDY TAPPING

Integrative Wellness, one-to-one sessions: www.tapoutstress.com/shop

To book public speaking engagements, trainings, and corporate coaching events, contact Mary Cassidy LLC Integrative Wellness at 406-223-2359.

BOOKS

Built to Last, by Jim Collins and Jerry I. Porras, New York, NY: HarperCollins, 2002.

Creating Affluence: The A-to-Z Steps to a Richer Life, by Deepak Chopra, San Rafael, CA: Amber-Allen Publishing, 2011.

Creating Affluence: Wealth Consciousness in the Field of All Possibilities, by Deepak Chopra, San Rafael, CA: New World Library, 1993.

The Secret, by Rhonda Byrne, New York, NY: Simon and Schuster, 2006, https://www.thesecret.tv/products/the-secret-book/.

The Success Principles: How to Get from Where You are to Where You Want to Be by Jack Canfield and Janet Switzer, New York, NY: HarperCollins, 2015.

The User's Manual for the Brain by Bob G. Bodenhamer and L. Michael Hall, Bethel, CT: Crown House Publishing, LLC, 2012.

WEBSITES

Brené Brown, research professor, author, brenebrown.com

Jack Canfield, transformational leader, *The Canfield Training Group*, jackcanfield.com

Dave Ramsey, financial transformation leader, daveramsey.com

OTHER TAPPING RESOURCES

Rita Freilinger Duncan, RN, LMT, Stress Relief Educator, www.taptochange.com

Christin McLeod, Personal Transformation Coach and Life Strategist, www.christinmcleod.com

Eutaptics FasterEFT trainings, Robert G. Smith, YouTube, https://www.youtube.com/user/HealingMagic

Faster Changes Transformational Life Coaching, www.fasterchanges.com

FasterEFT, www.fastereft.com

FasterEFT—The Ultimate Learning Kit by Robert G. Smith, Skills to Change Institute, ttps://fastereft.com/products/training/seminars/ultimate-learning-kit/

Heal Your Sexual Self seminar, Robert G. Smith, Skills to Change Institute, fastereft.com/events

OTHER RESOURCES

William Bengston, *Hands-on Healing: A Training Course in the Energy Cure* program, https://www.bengstonresearch.com/book-cd

Dave Ramsey, *Financial Peace University* course, https://www.daveramsey.com/courses

Tony Robbins, *Results Coaching* program, https://www.tonyrobbins.com/coaching/results-coaching/

Tony Robbins, *Ultimate Edge* program, https://www.tonyrobbins.com/ultimate-edge/

The Secret, movie, Rhonda Byrne and Paul Harrington (find it on Netflix, YouTube, Amazon Prime)

Headspace, meditation app, Headspace.com

Omvana, meditation app, Omvana.com

Notes

1. Brené Brown, https://brenebrown.com/. Last accessed Dec. 27, 2018.

2. "Dissociative Disorders," National Alliance on Mental Health, https://www.nami.org/Learn-More/Mental-Health-Conditions/Dissociative-Disorders. Last accessed Dec. 14, 2018.

3. TS Rao Sathyanarayana, et al., "The biochemistry of belief Indian," Indian Journal of Psychiatry, 2009; 51(4): 239–241, https://www.ncbi.nlm.nih.gov/pmc/articles/PMC2802367/.

4. Manuela Lenzen, "Feeling Our Emotions," interview with Antonio Damasio, Scientific American, April 2005; Mind 16(1): 14–15. https://www.scientificamerican.com/article/feeling-our-emotions/. Last accessed Dec. 14, 2018.

5. Bob G. Bodenhamer and L. Michael Hall, The User's Manual for the Brain, Bethel, CT: Crown House Publishing, LLC, 2012.

6. Study.com, Introduction to Psychology, "Reticular Activating System: Definition and Function," chapter 4, lesson 10, Sharon Linde,

instructor, www.study.com/academy/lesson/reticular-activating-system-definition-function.html. Last accessed Oct. 7, 2018.

7. PsycholoGenie, "What Is the Difference between Subconscious and Unconscious Mind?" July 14, 2017, https://psychologenie.com/difference-between-subconscious-unconscious-mind. Last accessed Dec. 13, 2018.

8. Robert Fritz, *Creating*, New York, NY: Fawcett Columbine Publishing, 1991.

9. Louise L. Hay, *Heal Your Body*, Carlsbad, CA: Hay House, Inc., 2007.

10. Brené Brown, "Shame v. Guilt," https://brenebrown.com/blog/2013/01/14/shame-v-guilt/. Last accessed Jan. 1, 2019.

Ingram Content Group UK Ltd.
Milton Keynes UK
UKHW022330160623
423577UK00013B/1095